Step-by-Step

PATIOS & DECKS

Step-by-Step

PATIOS & DECKS

Penny Swift and Janek Szymanowski

AURA BOOKS

NEW HOLLAND

First published in the UK in 1994 by
New Holland (Publishers) Ltd
37 Connaught Street, London W2 2AZ
in association with Aura Books plc

ISBN 1 85368 338 8

Editors Jenny Barrett and Coral Walker
Project coordinator Annlerie van Rooyen
Designer Petal Muller
Cover designer Jenny Frost
Assistant designer Clarence Clarke
Illustrator Clarence Clarke
Indexer and proofreader Sandie Vahl

Typesetting by Struik DTP
Reproduction by Unifoto (Pty) Ltd
Printed and bound by Tien Wah Press (Pte.), Singapore

CONTENTS

INTRODUCTION 6

BUILDING BASICS 10

BUILDING TECHNIQUES 19

DECKS 28

PATIOS 46

STEPS AND PATHS 66

OVERHEADS AND SCREENS 79

FINISHING TOUCHES 89

LIST OF SUPPLIERS 94

GLOSSARY 95

INDEX 96

INTRODUCTION

Set on a steep slope with sea views, this deck encircling a spa was professionally designed and built.

Whether your garden is new or well-established, creating an outdoor living area will not only be rewarding but have both practical and aesthetic benefits too. There are numerous possibilities for decks, courtyards and patios, all of which may be designed in just about any style to meet your specific requirements. A wide range of materials may be used, depending on availability and your building skills.

Anybody aiming to get the maximum use from their property will probably want to explore improvement possibilities for both house and garden. Just as we relish the warmth of a roaring fire indoors during the winter months, in fine weather, there is nothing better than spending time outdoors. A well-planned patio or deck will allow you to do just this, and enable you to establish an indoor-outdoor lifestyle, whenever the weather permits.

Where doors open on to the garden, it is advisable to have some sort of hard surface, in the form of a patio or verandah,

steps or pathway, to prevent people from tramping dirt inside. You may also be able to accommodate seating and planting. If you want to create an outdoor area above ground level, perhaps for alfresco meals, or if your house is on sloping ground, a timber deck will often be a good solution.

Paved patios and terraces may also be located away from the house, in secluded corners or shady niches. You may prefer to consider the possibility of a low-level deck somewhere in your garden, or perhaps to construct a timber floor around your swimming pool or hot tub.

There are numerous options, many of which you will be able to tackle yourself with basic skills. This book will provide you with plenty of ideas for building and remodelling every kind of outdoor space. Comprehensive information is given on tools and building techniques, as well as on structural materials for the floor surface, overhead arrangements, seating, and simple screens and walls.

Projects are presented in a step-by-step format which is easy to follow, and which aims to help you to achieve a professional finish. Materials are also discussed so that you can cost each job before you begin and make sure that you have everything at hand when you start work.

Finally, there are the ever-important finishing touches: lighting, freestanding furniture, built-in seating, plants and containers will help to make your deck or patio unique and attractive.

PLANNING

There is no doubt that proper planning pays off. Not only does it facilitate budgeting, helping you estimate accurately and, where necessary, trim costs and avoid expensive mistakes, but it is also the key to creating a successful outdoor feature which you can enjoy to the full.

Getting started

Before you do anything else, establish what needs the deck or patio should fulfil. Then decide on its location and the design which best suits your requirements.

Your lifestyle will play an important role in the decisions you make at the planning stage. If you entertain a lot and want to use the deck or patio for alfresco meals, accessiblity to the house will be a major factor. If, on the other hand, you want a quiet retreat where you can sit and read or relax in peace, site the patio away from the house and any other established outdoor living areas.

At the same time, you will also have to consider maintenance, the weather, views, privacy and safety. As far as the structure itself goes, some materials require more maintenance than others (see pages 25 and 36), so consider how much time and effort you are prepared to put into this. If you enjoy gardening, you will probably be quite content to potter about tending pot plants and flowers, rather than growing hardy shrubs or establishing low-maintenance beds around your outdoor living area. Although built-in seating is useful and practical, you may prefer to have moveable furniture which can be rearranged easily. Either way, if you have cushions on the seats, bear in mind that covers will probably have to be cleaned regularly, and also make sure that you have easy access to a storage place.

Before finally deciding on a location, spend some time in the garden and take note of prevailing winds, and of where shade falls in the garden at different times of day. Although you could use umbrellas or erect overhead shelter to provide some shade in an area constantly in the sun, outdoor areas exposed to strong wind will always be unpleasant as little can be done to rectify the situation.

Decide whether there is anything in the garden, or visible from the garden, which you would prefer to conceal. You could position your deck or patio so that it faces a pleasing view or a pretty, well-established part of the garden.

If the area you choose is overlooked by neighbours, or faces on to a busy street, family and friends may well prefer to sit elsewhere, and your efforts and expenditure will be wasted. If, however, you cannot site the deck or patio anywhere else, pay special attention to screens and overhead structures to provide privacy and shade.

Also make sure that both the deck or patio and the access to and from the house are safe to use. Choose a non-slip surface for the floor of your deck or patio, and if an existing pathway tends to become slippery in wet weather, consider resurfacing it. When you design a balustrade, make the height and spacing of the railings safe for small children. Also check that outside lighting is adequate.

The role of professionals

While most of the projects featured in this book are well within the scope of DIY enthusiasts with basic building skills, some require a greater level of expertise.

If you find it difficult to conceptualise, ask a landscape architect or garden designer to help you. Even if your regional authority does not require plans, sketches prepared by a professional person will be an invaluable aid during the planning stages, particularly when quantifying materials and costing the project. Some landscape architects and garden designers will also be prepared to assist in the capacity of project manager, overseeing the whole operation.

If formal plans are required for a screen wall, barbecue or pergola, you could approach an architect or landscaper to supply them. However, engaging a draughtsman could save you money, or, if you are going to hire a building contractor anyway, you could ask him to organise plans for you. Draughtsmen are not trained in design, however, so you should have a clear idea of what you want before you hire one or brief a contractor.

Brick paving and multilevel decking have been used together to landscape a sloping garden.

A wooden jetty is purely functional for those living on this waterside property.

A simple low-level deck has been constructed to double as a diving-board, while a brick-paved patio and lawn lie alongside the pool.

Brick, tiles and wood have been combined creatively around an angled swimming pool leading from a house.

If you are not going to do the work yourself, a more cost-effective option than a contractor when it comes to building is often to hire qualified subcontractors – bricklayers, plasterers, carpenters and pavers all have special skills that could take time to master. Many building contractors hire subcontractors themselves, adding on to their fee if they are to supervise and take responsibility for the finished job. If, however, you plan to oversee the job personally, study the section on Building Basics carefully.

Determining the cost

Once you have decided where you are going to site your deck or patio and roughly what your needs are, you will have to choose the design and materials that appeal to you most. Price is almost always a factor, especially if you have a tight budget. Careful planning is the key to cost control, and is also the best way to cut down on wastage.

Using the step-by-step projects as a guide, list everything you need, including any tools you may have to hire or buy. The quantities of materials specified for the projects in this book are just estimates, but for accurate budgeting it pays to be as precise as possible (see pages 12-18).

Calculating the number of bricks, blocks, pavers, tiles and so on which you will need is reasonably simple (see pages 12-13), but quantifying items like cement, sand, stone, tile adhesive and grout is more difficult. For instance, wastage of mortar used for laying bricks or blocks will vary according to the competence of the builder, and extra concrete will be used if foundations and footings are wider or deeper than the dimensions specified. Timber purchased will also depend on standard lengths available in your area. You will often have to buy more than is needed; however you can usually estimate wastage in advance.

If you do not have a lot of free time, consider employing someone else to do at least some of the work for you. Make sure that you assess the fees of any professionals or subcontractors accurately, and if possible, agree on a price for the whole job rather than paying a daily rate, especially as you could easily underestimate the time it will take to complete the project.

If you find that your budget will not cover all predicted expenses, you may be able to cut costs by using alternative materials or by doing more of the work yourself. Often the best solution is to do the job in stages; for instance, you could build a patio now and a timber pergola later; or construct a deck and add finishing touches, like seating, when finances permit.

An attractive, tiled patio, extending around a pool, features several different seating areas.

This timber-floored verandah is a perfect place to sit and enjoy magnificent views.

BUILDING BASICS

Before you tackle a building project such as a deck or patio, you will need to know what materials are required as well as what is available in your area. You must also ensure that you have all the tools you will need for the project.

TOOLS

Most do-it-yourselfers have some tools of their own, but if you have to buy tools, always get the best quality you can afford; they will last longer and make the task at hand easier. However, instead of buying special equipment, you could hire items like compacting machines, augers, angle grinders and power saws from a hiring service; your local classified telephone directory should list such companies.

Retractable tape measures, used to set out all projects and to measure both materials and the building area, are available in various lengths. Good quality steel tapes have a locking mechanism, so one can use them without assistance.

A *builder's line*, or even ordinary string, is essential for setting out and for ensuring that brickwork and paving is straight and level. Attach it to *pegs* in the ground, or wind it around L-shaped *corner blocks* and hook them on to the ends of brickwork (see page 22). Although metal pegs are available commercially, both pegs and corner blocks are easy to make from wood. A *chalk line* is a retractable string coated in chalk. It is used to mark straight lines on any surface, for lining up decking slats or tiles, positioning ledgers, and marking cutting lines, for instance.

Squares, particularly steel squares, are vital for checking right angles, and usually have metric and/or imperial measurements marked off on them. The types that are most commonly used for building are builder's squares and carpenter's squares. A smaller combination square, which incorporates a spirit level vial, can be useful for minor building projects and carpentry. A simple home-made wooden square is a practical aid when setting out a rectangular patio or structure. It is made by cutting three lengths of timber in the ratio 3:4:5 – for example, 0.9 m, 1.2 m and 1.5 m (3 ft, 4 ft and 5 ft) – and nailing them together to form a right-angled triangle.

A *straightedge* is simply a straight length of wood used to level concrete slabs or sand beds. It is often used together with a spirit level. Marked off at intervals equal to the height of a single brick or block plus mortar joint, it will double as a *gauge rod*, for checking that brick courses are equal.

A spirit level is indispensable for ensuring that all surfaces are horizontal or plumb.

Levels are also indispensable. The most common type is the ordinary spirit level which has a horizontal and a vertical indicator. There are various sizes, but for the sake of accuracy it is best to opt for the longest you can manage; 1.2 m (4 ft) is a handy length. Attached to a builder's line, a line level is used during setting out or to check that walls or brick pillars are progressing evenly. A water level, another home-made tool, is invaluable when one is working on a slope or levelling the tops of poles or timber posts (see pages 43 and 85). Made from a piece of transparent tubing, it may also be used instead of a line level when building pillars. A *plumb bob* is a weight attached to a length of string, and is used to check vertical surfaces. The more expensive types have a built-in line reel.

Spacers are used to ensure equal joints between tiles. They are made of plastic or metal and are available in various shapes and sizes. Although some are left permanently in place, most are removed

before grouting. A narrow length of wood can be used instead when laying rigid paving, or small pieces of wood for decking slats.

Spades and *shovels* are used for digging foundations and mixing concrete, mortar and plaster or render. The slightly rounded shape of a shovel makes it better suited for shifting soil and mixing. A *pick* is useful when excavating hard or heavy clay ground, while one can hire an *auger* or post-hole borer (which may be either a hand tool or power-driven) to bore holes in the ground. This is useful if you are sinking poles directly into the soil or using tube forms to contain concrete footings for post anchors.

Wheelbarrows are indispensable for transporting materials, and a builder's wheelbarrow (with steep sides) may also be used for mixing concrete. Builder's buckets, empty drums and large paint cans are all useful for measuring materials by volume (see page 13).

Compactors are useful when paving, laying blocks or casting a slab for floor surfaces. Plate vibrators will compact the ground or fill (broken bricks, stone and so on) to form a firm sub-base for concrete or paving. Rubber-line rollers are commonly used to level some types of paving after it has been laid. A *punner* or *ramming tool* may be used instead of a compactor. To make your own, fill a 5 litre (1 gal) tin with

An angle grinder is used to cut a thick tile.

concrete and set a pole in the centre. Alternatively, attach a solid block of wood or a metal plate to a pole.

A *cold chisel*, which has a much narrower blade than a bolster, may be used for chipping out existing brickwork and plaster, or when removing old paving bricks previously mortared into position.

Angle grinders are useful for cutting bricks and tiles, and *block splitters* for halving some precast concrete products. Various *tile-cutting machines* are also available.

Concrete mixers, which may be electrically powered or driven by petrol or diesel, are a welcome aid when large quantities of concrete or mortar are to be mixed. These machines are available in several sizes from most hire shops.

Mortarboards and *screedboards* are handy for holding small quantities of mortar and plaster or render, but they are not really essential for DIY projects.

Trowels are used for both bricklaying and plastering or rendering. A small trowel may be used to neaten facebrick surfaces, although special *pointing tools* are also available. Corner trowels (for inside and outside corners) are used where two plastered surfaces meet at right angles. *Jointers*, used to fashion a variety of different joints in facebrick walls, are not really necessary for garden brickwork. Wooden and metal *floats* are used to smooth plaster and the screed laid over concrete slabs or floors.

Hammers are essential. An ordinary claw hammer is invaluable for nailing timber and extracting nails. Brick hammers have a sharp chisel end instead

of a claw, and are used for cutting bricks. When used with a *bolster* (broad chisel), hefty club hammers are also useful for this purpose. A *rubber mallet*, which looks like a hammer but has a heavy rubber-topped head, is used to knock paving bricks or blocks, concrete slabs and cobbles into place when they are not quite level.

A tenon saw is handy for cutting small pieces of wood.

Saws are essential for all woodwork. Even if you order exact lengths of timber, there is bound to be some cutting to do. There are many types of handsaw, including a general purpose bowsaw, useful for sawing logs and wooden poles, and a hacksaw, which may also be used for cutting metal, such as bolts. A ripsaw may be used to saw along or with the grain of most woods, while a crosscut saw works best across the grain; smaller panel saws do both, but are designed for fine-grained timber. A tenon saw or back saw will cope with most small jobs and is invaluable for shaping wood for mortise-and-tenon joints. Electric saws will speed up the

operation. The two most useful types are circular saws, which may be fitted with a range of blades and will make smooth, flat cuts at any angle, or jigsaws, which may be used to create curved edges.

A *bradawl* is used to pierce wood before screwing in very small screws.

An electric drill is a good investment for the DIY enthusiast.

Drills are indispensable for any woodwork project. The cheapest type is a hand drill or wheel brace, but it can be of somewhat limited use. An electric drill is more efficient, and you will be able to use it for a much wider range of projects. Ideally, invest in a machine with variable speeds. Some also have a hammer action, although this is only necessary if you will be drilling into very hard surfaces such as concrete lintels. Battery-operated drills are also available. You will need wood bits for drilling into timber, and masonry bits to make holes in brickwork or concrete. A countersink bit will enable you to create a tapered hole for screws.

Chisels, especially those with a bevelled edge, are for paring, cutting and chopping out wood joints. There are various types, including a mortise chisel for shaping mortise-and-tenon joints. An electric *router* is ideal for cutting grooves and rebates, and for creating chamfered edges on timber. It may also be used to form decorative profiles on pergolas.

Screwdrivers are an integral part of any woodworker's toolkit. Ideally, you should buy a selection of screwdrivers in different sizes, with both flat blades and Phillips (cross-point) drivers. For ease of handling, a spiral ratchet screwdriver, with different positions and a reverse action designed for removing screws, will prove invaluable.

A claw hammer and a corner clamp in use.

A circular saw makes a smooth, clean cut.

Spanners are required for tightening nuts and bolts. Several types are available, including flat, socket and ring spanners, as well as adjustable shifting spanners. *Pliers* can sometimes be used instead of a spanner, although care must be taken not to damage the bolt.

Clamps are invaluable when building a timber deck, as they enable you to keep lengths of wood firmly together while you drill and fasten them. Long sash clamps may also be used to help straighten decking beams if the timber bows slightly.

Rasps and *files* are useful for planing and filing small lengths of timber. An electric *plane* will speed up the process, and most models will enable you to tackle rebates and chamfered edges as well.

Sanders are invaluable machines even if you are working with timber which has already been 'planed all round' (PAR). The cheapest option is to fit a sanding disc to a drill, but while this is useful for sanding very rough wood, it is difficult to avoid marking the timber. A belt sander will level planed or reasonably rough wood, while a more compact orbital sander, with a vibrating sanding pad, will give a good, smooth finish to the surface.

Work-benches are useful if there is cutting or predrilling to be done, or if you are screwing together timbers before positioning them. A workshop at home is ideal, but a spacious toolshed with a workshop area can also be used. Compact, portable and adjustable work-benches are invaluable, with vices and sash clamps for holding timber while you drill and screw it.

MATERIALS

The most common materials you will work with are cement, sand and stone for concrete slabs and foundations, bricks and mortar for walls and paving, and timber for decks. You will also need a selection of nails, screws and bolts, and, if you are constructing pillars for a pergola, metal strapping and reinforcing rods. Other possibilities for the patio floor are discussed in the section on Patios, on pages 48-50.

Bricks and blocks

Made from clay or precast concrete, bricks and blocks for walls and paving are available in a range of colours. Most paving bricks have a lightly textured surface, while those used for building are available in a much wider variety of textures, both as facebricks and for a plastered finish.

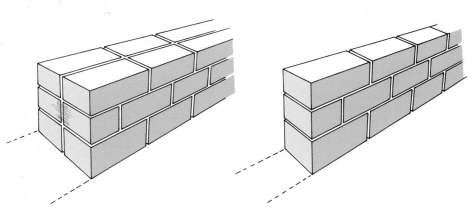

A one-brick wall.

A half-brick wall.

The most common type of brick is rectangular, and varies in thickness (or height) from approximately 50 mm (2 in) for paving only, to not more than 73 mm (3 in) for bricklaying and paving. In spite of slight differences in width and length, when calculating quantities, it is safe to assume that you will need 55 standard bricks for each square metre (46 bricks per square yard) of half-brick walling, which will be about 106 mm (4 in) thick. For a square metre of paving, you can count on using up to 45 bricks or blocks

(38 pavers per square yard). These figures, as well as those given in the projects, allow for some wastage.

While clay and concrete are both used to manufacture flat-sided pavers, some concrete bricks and blocks are shaped to fit into each other. For instance, interlocking road stones, with zig-zag edges, bond particularly well on steep slopes, making them a suitable option for driveways, while others fit together like puzzle pieces. Some types come in different shapes and sizes and are designed so that the corner

A selection of bricks, blocks and pavers made from both clay and concrete.

of each block fits into the adjacent block. They can even be laid so that grass or a ground cover can grow between the units, which remain firmly interlocked. Hollow turf blocks have a similar effect.

Large, hollow concrete blocks, which are manufactured in several sizes, are useful for building garden structures, but they should be rendered for a more pleasing finish. Reconstituted or reconstructed stone blocks are a more attractive option. Moulded from concrete and tinted with a coloured pigment, they are available in several sizes, and are laid in a random fashion to create the effect of cut stone. Perforated breeze blocks are another option, particularly for screen walls.

To work out how many blocks you will need for building, calculate the surface area of the wall(s) to be built, and divide this by the area of the side of one block plus a 10 mm (½ in) mortar joint. If you are working with blocks of different sizes, the simplest solution is to add the areas of each kind and use equal numbers of each.

Cement

Used for concrete, mortar and plaster (or render), cement is commonly sold in 50 kg (110 lb) bags. Although there are various types, ordinary Portland cement is available internationally and is the DIY builder's first choice.

Remember that cement hardens when mixed with water, and that it should therefore be stored away from damp. If you do not have a platform of some kind, put plastic under the bags and stack a maximum of 12 bags on top of one another, preferably under cover. If cement is left outdoors and it rains or there is heavy dew, even plastic will do little to prevent the material from hardening or becoming lumpy. Ideally, cement should not be kept for longer than three months. If it is offered for sale at a very reduced price, it could be because it is old stock which will not have the strength of the freshly manufactured product.

The quantity of cement required will depend on the strength of the mixture, which will vary according to the type of work you are doing. For instance, a suitable mortar mix for garden projects consists of cement and sand in a 1:4 ratio, measured by volume. For this you can count on using one bag of cement for every 200 standard bricks in a half-brick wall. More will be needed if you are building a one-brick wall with a double skin of brickwork; and here it is safe to assume that you will need one bag for every 150 bricks. The same mix ratio may be used for plaster or render, and a single

A DIY builder loads sand, stone and cement into a small, manually operated concrete mixer.

bag of cement will enable you to cover about 12 m² (14 sq yd) of wall, provided that the finished covering is approximately 10-15 mm (about ½ in) thick.

Water

Water is a vital ingredient when working with cement. As a rule, any water suitable for drinking may be used for building.

Sand

An important ingredient in concrete, mortar and plaster mixes, sand is also used on its own as the bedding material for paving. For a newcomer to DIY projects, it may seem strange that you should have to buy it, especially if you live near a beach or dunes or alongside a river where sandy soil is plentiful. However, for conservation reasons it is illegal in many places to remove sand from beaches and dunes. Furthermore, it is essential that sand used for building is clean, free of all vegetable matter and without a clay content – factors which will be taken care of by any reputable supplier. The actual source of the sand is not a reliable guide to its quality. The best building sands are evenly graded, and contain particles of different sizes.

Nevertheless, you may be guided by the fact that river sand is generally quite clean and free from clay, and contains hard

particles which aid the workability of concrete. Pit sand is usually well graded, although it often contains a lot of clay and has to be professionally washed. If beach sand is properly processed, so that it is salt-free and does not contain shell particles, it may be used for building. Although clean dune sand is often suitable, avoid using very fine sands, like wind-blown sand from desert areas or mine-dump sand which has been sieved a lot. In addition to these natural sands, specially manufactured crushed sand, which is also washed and graded, is suitable for concrete work.

In general, the sand used for making concrete should be reasonably coarse. It may be classified as 'sharp' sand, or simply building sand. Sand used for mortar and plaster should be softer, with more fine material (known as 'fines'). Some ordinary building sands are quite suitable for mortar, although it is a good idea to add hydrated builder's lime or a plasticiser to make the mixture more malleable and improve its water-retentive quality. This will in turn increase its resistance to cracking as it hardens. Coarse concrete sand is not suitable for plaster or render, although plaster sand may be used to make mortar for bricklaying. In some areas suppliers add lime to sand and it is sold as

A charming, brick-paved patio overlooks the surrounding countryside. Canvas blinds may be rolled down at the sides for additional shelter.

'plaster sand' or 'lime sand'. For flexible paving (see pages 52-53), the bedding sand should be coarser than that used between the joints.

Although sand is widely available in 50 kg (110 lb) bags, it is more sensible to buy it by volume from a builder's merchant or general transport company when a large quantity is needed. The smallest load most will deliver is 0.5 m³ or ½ cu yd.

Using a standard cement:sand ratio of 1:4 for mixing mortar and plaster or render, you will need about 125 kg (275 lb) or 100 litres (22 gal) of sand for every 100 bricks you are going to lay. When tackling more extensive brickwork, base your estimates on 1 m³ (1⅓ cu yd) per 1,000 bricks. For plasterwork or

rendering, you should not need more than 16 kg of sand for each square metre (30 lb per square yard).

The amount required for foundations and slabs will depend on the mix specified – the more sand you add, the weaker the concrete will be. For 40 mm (1½ in) thick bedding under paving, you will need 1 m³ for every 25 m² (1 cu yd per 25 sq yd).

However, when working out the volume of sand you will need, it is useful to know that 100 litres (22 gal) weighs roughly 135 kg (298 lb). Bear in mind, though, that mathematical calculations will never be completely accurate as sands differ and their moisture content varies, sometimes affecting the weight considerably. If you are in a very windy area, you will also experience more wastage than normal; it

helps to keep the sand covered with plastic weighed down with bricks, or to keep it damp, to prevent it from blowing away.

Stone

Referred to in the building trade as 'aggregate', stone used to make concrete is frequently crushed and sieved to attain what suppliers call 'single-size' stone. If suitable river pebbles are available, these may be used instead.

For DIY projects, a medium-sized crushed stone is a sensible choice, as it is the easiest to handle. Gradings of stone may vary, but 19 mm (¾ in) and 13.2 mm (½ in) are the most usual size.

Like sand, aggregate is sold in bags or by volume, and the quantity required will depend on both the mix you are using and the area to be concreted. The size of the stone will also affect the proportions. For instance, low-strength concrete, mixed in a cement:sand:stone ratio of 1:4:4 is quite adequate for most foundations and footings in the garden. If you are building more substantial walls though, the ratio should be altered to 1:3:4 or even 1:3:3, and if the smaller stone is used, change these ratios to 1:4:3 and 1:3:2 respectively. Bear in mind that all quantities given in the projects in this book are calculated for the larger stone size.

Lime and plasticiser

You should be able to find lime at any outlet that sells cement. Sold in 25 kg (55 lb) bags, hydrated builder's lime is invaluable for improving the plasticity and cohesiveness of cement mixtures – especially when the sand lacks fines. Furthermore, hardened mortar and plaster are less likely to crack if lime is used.

For garden work, a bag of lime may be added to every bag of cement. Even though it will increase the yield slightly, do not alter the cement:sand proportions already given.

Proprietary plasticisers are sometimes used as an alternative for lime in mortar mixes, or to make concrete more pliable. Usually 50 ml (2 fl oz) of plasticiser is added to every 50 kg (110 lb) of cement. Quicklime (calcium oxide) and agricultural lime are not suitable for building work.

Timber

The wood used to build decks, pergolas and other similar structures should be durable and structurally sound. Ensure that it is suitable for the project you are tackling and never buy wood with obvious defects. If inferior wood is used to build a deck or to make seating on a patio, you will soon have to spend time and money repairing or even replacing it.

Of course the species and the cut of the wood selected (see page 32) will depend to a large extent on what is available locally, as well as on the structure you are building. Poles, for instance, are suitable for some pergolas and for the uprights of a deck, while sawn timber will be required for seating, beams, joists and decking slats.

Furthermore, different species have different qualities, and you should investigate these before choosing your wood. The classification of timber into hardwoods and softwoods can be especially confusing. The definition is a botanical one – broadleafed species being loosely grouped as hardwoods, and conifers as softwoods – and has nothing to do with the durability, strength or

Various types of timber may be used to build decks and overhead structures. It may simply be sealed, like this two-level spa deck, or painted like the pergola in the background.

'hard' and 'soft' qualities of the wood. Balsa wood, for instance, is very soft and easy to carve, but it is a hardwood; on the other hand, redwood is a softwood, but is reasonably strong and hard, and it is favoured for deck-building because of its resistance to decay.

In addition, you will find that wood sawn from different parts of the tree will have different qualities. For instance, heartwood, from the centre of the tree, is more resistant to decay, while sapwood, from near the bark, is porous and will absorb preservatives and other chemicals more efficiently.

It is advisable to stack timber at least 300 mm (12 in) off the ground, as well as to protect it with a tarpaulin or plastic covering if it is to be stored outdoors before construction begins.

Typical defects found in sawn timber include, from top to bottom, knots, bowing, cupping and twisting.

A tiny low-level deck made from karri leads from a charming bedroom in a small log cabin.

Poles For building projects you will need poles which are reasonably regular in size from top to bottom. For this reason it is usually more sensible to opt for those that have been machined to a smooth surface, rather than logs that have simply been debarked. As poles are relatively narrow in relation to their length, not all tree species are suitable. Two woods which are sometimes available commercially as poles are pine and eucalyptus (gum). Whatever you choose, though, it is essential that the timber has been impregnated with a suitable preservative (see below).

Sawn timber The primary material used for building decks is sawn timber. Various types are suitable, although your choice will be subject to availability and cost. Some of the more popular wood species are listed on page 32.

Most of the sawn timber used for garden structures is purchased planed all round (PAR), making it reasonably smooth and ready to work with. A light sanding is all that is required to finish it off prior to painting or sealing. You can, of course,

buy rough-cut timber, but if it is going to be visible after construction you will have to plane it down yourself.

Wood is graded according to strength and appearance. Whatever kind you buy, get the best quality available – you will inevitably encounter problems with substandard wood (see page 15). If it bows or even twists slightly, you will have trouble ensuring that beams, joists and so on lie straight and level. In this case, you may have to bridge and block the timbers (see pages 34-35) or use clamps to pull them straight while you work. If decking slats cup, the sides will turn upwards, resulting in an uneven deck floor. Large knots and splitting will look ugly and threaten the stability of the structure as a whole. For this reason it makes sense to reject wood with any of these defects.

Standard sizes of sawn timber are fairly universal, although there is some variation. When ordering planks, beams and so on for projects, it is not always necessary to buy pieces of timber identical in size to those specified, although some cutting measurements will have to be adjusted

accordingly. If you wish, timber can be specially milled and planed to size, but this could increase your costs considerably.

Laminated timber This is manufactured by gluing strips of wood together under pressure; finger-joints (with a zig-zagged finish) are used to increase the length of the timber. Although more expensive, laminated timber boards are more stable and considerably stronger than those sawn from a single log, so when constructing a deck or pergola with very long beams, it may be best to use laminated timber.

Preservatives Any timber used for outdoor structures must be properly processed in the factory. Since moisture evaporates from the freshly sawn wood, it must first be dried to prevent it from shrinking. Even though some heartwoods are naturally resistant to decay and infestation, they should also be treated with a preservative to safeguard against insects and rot.

Most of the preservatives available for DIY use will not penetrate the wood thoroughly, so while they are useful for painting freshly cut ends and bolt holes, it is advisable to use factory-treated timber for all major structures.

Even if you are not treating the timber yourself, it is advisable to be aware of the types of preservative used. There are three basic types – the coal-tar creosotes, organic solvents and water-based types.

Creosote is probably the cheapest and best-known preservative, and is one many DIY builders use. Although suitable for outdoor use and for coating wood which will be buried in the ground, creosote is toxic to plants and causes some materials, including shadecloth, to rot. In addition, it is oily, has a strong smell, and cannot be overcoated with any other finish.

Organic solvent preservatives have fungicidal and insecticidal properties which protect outdoor timber. However, treated wood which is to be buried in the ground should be given extra protection with something like bitumen, a waterproofing compound sold in various forms. Most of these preservatives are odourless, although PCP (pentachlorophenol) has an unpleasant smell. Some types are toxic, and some leave a slightly oily residue which can affect surface finishes.

All water-based preservatives can easily be overcoated, but like the organic solvent preservatives, will not adequately protect timber which is buried underground. Most are odourless and colourless, except for CCA (chromated copper arsenate) which gives the timber a distinctly green tinge.

There is a wide choice of nails, screws, bolts and other hardware which may be used in the construction of decks, patios and related structures.

Finishes These days preservatives often contain a finish as well, but many basic preservatives will simply protect wood from infestation and rot, making it essential to protect the wood from weathering by oiling, varnishing or painting.

Timber experts often advocate water-repellant oil-type finishes as they soak into the wood, feeding and protecting it. While some builders simply use linseed oil on very hard woods (balau and teak, for example), specially formulated wood dressings will protect timber against weather, rot and insect attack. Since they are not resistant to sunlight, however, it is necessary to recoat the wood once or twice a year.

If varnish is to be used, choose a product that is both weatherproof and resistant to ultraviolet light. Alternatively, you may prefer to use paint. Various products are suitable, and the wood should be prepared according to the manufacturer's instructions. Although it will eventually deteriorate, and the wood will have to be repainted from time to time, paint will enable you both to introduce colour and to coordinate outside areas.

The nuts and bolts

You will need a selection of nails, screws and bolts for all the projects, as well as reinforcing rods and metal strapping if you are constructing brick or block pillars. Various special connectors are also useful.

Use fasteners and connectors which will not rust, especially if they will be visible. Brass (which may be a bit expensive), stainless steel, aluminium and galvanised or anodised metal are all suitable.

Nails Sold by weight rather than by number, nails come in many forms suitable for a variety of jobs. While most nails have round or oval shanks, some are roughened or twisted.

Those you are most likely to use for decking and patio structures include ordinary wire nails, which can be used for reasonably rough carpentry, and box nails, which have broad heads. Ring-shanked nails are useful for securing corrugated iron and fibrecement sheeting to roof structures, but they should otherwise be avoided as they can be cumbersome and very difficult to remove.

Staples If you are using a staple gun to attach awning material, you will need special heavy-duty staples. After stapling, hammer them in lightly.

Screws Indispensable for any project involving woodwork, screws are made from various metals. Once again, it is always good practice to choose brass or anodised metal screws as they will not rust.

Screws come in various gauges which indicate the diameter of the shank, as well as a range of lengths. The thread usually extends a little more than halfway up the length of the screw, and should be completely embedded in the bottom piece of wood. Self-tapping screws can be driven directly into the wood or into a smaller pilot hole.

While ordinary screws have a single slot in the head, Phillips screws have a cross-shaped slot, and are often countersunk, with a flat top and sloping sides. Phillips screws are commonly used to secure decking slats. Self-tapping coach screws have a flat, hexagonal head and are tightened with a spanner.

In the case of this deck, constructed on a steep slope, the nuts and bolts are not obvious when the project is complete.

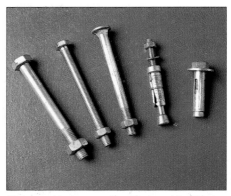

Hexagonal bolts, a cuphead bolt and Rawl bolts.

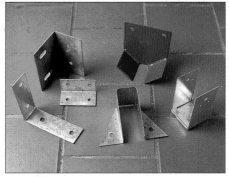

Three angle brackets, a pole hanger, a truss hanger and a post anchor.

Bolts A variety of bolts may be used for the substructure of a deck. They include cuphead bolts (coach bolts) which have a rounded head and a short thread, and hexagonal bolts, which have a hexagonal head and sometimes a thread extending the full length of the shaft. All are used with nuts and washers.

When attaching timber to bricks and mortar, the best option is to use Rawl bolts. These heavy-duty fixers are made from metal, part of which expands to anchor the bolt securely in the wall.

Special connectors A host of special connectors, including joist hangers, post anchors and angle brackets, make life easy for the DIY builder. Most are made from galvanised iron to resist rust, and can usually be painted if they are primed first.

Joist hangers are ideal for pergolas or decks which are attached to a wall. Some have metal prongs that are hammered into the timber itself, others are secured to the wood with screws.

Post anchors (post anchor bases) come in various shapes and sizes, but the function of all of them is the same: to secure a load-bearing post above ground level.

Angle brackets come in different thicknesses of metal, and are available with pre-drilled holes. Most are L-shaped or T-shaped, although some are set at other angles.

When using poles, one of the simplest joining devices is a specially formed galvanised metal cradle which is designed specifically for poles. This rigid connector has claws and spikes as well as holes for nails and screws. Another connector features a series of galvanised steel brackets which will enable you to join poles at any angle, although it is not universally available. For attaching poles to a wall, you can use a specially shaped bracket which is bolted to the wall.

Reinforcing metal Special metal reinforcing devices of various kinds are available, although it is also quite acceptable to use ordinary metal rods to strengthen pillars and piers. A sturdy metal mesh, which is sold in a roll, can be very useful for reinforcing steps or the brickwork above arches, niches and holes in walls. Galvanised metal strapping can be used for securing pergola beams, but must be built into the structure (see page 85).

BUILDING TECHNIQUES

Before you build even the simplest deck or patio, it is essential to master a few basic techniques. It makes sense to practise those you have never attempted prior to starting work on the project itself. However, the skills required for all the projects in this book are well within the scope of any handyman or DIY enthusiast.

Fundamental principles

No matter what materials you are using, there are certain fundamental principles which must be adhered to when tackling any building project – if you are to achieve a professional finish, your workmanship must be square, level and plumb.

Square For a structure to be square, all materials must be joined or laid so that the surfaces are at 90° to each other. If this is not done, poles and pillars may be lopsided and paving uneven, and gaps may form at the joints. If a deck is acutely angled, or if sections of a railing are joined diagonally, for instance, the timbers will obviously not be square, although the angle must nevertheless be accurate.

The simplest and most reliable way to check an angle during construction is to use a square (see page 10). An adjustable carpenter's or combination square will enable you to create a variety of angles. When setting out a patio or deck, the best way to check for square is to use the 3:4:5 method. If you are working alone, you can make a large wooden triangle (also called a square) with the lengths of the sides in this ratio, and use it to check the corners you have pegged out. For more accurate results, though, work with a second person and measure each side of the area you are setting out. Measure 4 m (12 ft) in one direction and 3 m (9 ft) at right angles to this, and the distance between these two points should be exactly 5 m (15 ft). If it is not, adjust the lines.

Level Another important building principle is that all surfaces must be level. However, this does not necessarily mean that they must be exactly horizontal – in some cases you will need to create a slight gradient for drainage purposes.

Various tools are used to check that surfaces are level. Ordinary spirit levels, combination squares and line levels (see

page 10) all incorporate one or more vials which are simple to read. If the bubble is centred, the surface you are working on is level. For a slight slope, the bubble should be slightly off-centre. To create an exact gradient, a block of wood can be placed under a straightedge and the spirit level read normally. If, for instance, the straightedge is 2 m (6 ft) long, you will need a small block of wood 50 mm (2 in) thick to get a 1:40 run-off. A spirit level is used in almost every part of the building operation, from throwing foundations, to screeding and paving floor surfaces, and

A line level and a metal builder's square are both useful for setting out a deck.

A simple, home-made water level is invaluable for aligning timbers when building a deck.

building walls, pillars or timber structures. A more compact combination square is useful for smaller woodwork projects, while a line level may be used to check levels above ground and to ensure that brickwork is progressing evenly.

Cheapest of all is the water level, an ingenious tool which may be used instead of a line level. Based on the principle that water finds its own level, it is an invaluable aid when erecting the upright posts or pillars of decks and pergolas. It is also the only method you can use if the structure extends around a corner. All you need in

When setting out, a good way to check right angles is to use the 3:4:5 method.

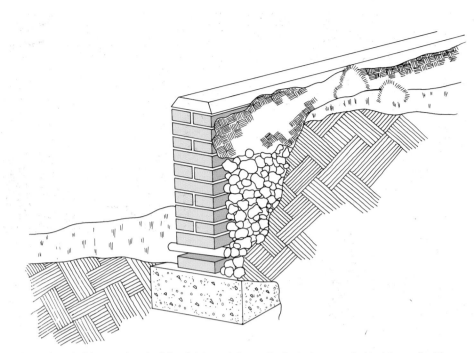

Drainage is a vital factor when building brick retaining walls. Pack the space behind the wall with hardcore and stones, and insert drainage pipes at the base of the wall.

order to make a water level is a piece of transparent tubing. Fill it with water and attach it or have someone hold it to one of the posts at the required height. Then take the other end and hold it against a second post. You will know that the post you are measuring is the correct height if the level of the water remains at the point you have marked on the first post.

Plumb Just as horizontal surfaces must be level, so too must all vertical surfaces, whether they are built from timber or bricks and mortar. Since a spirit level often has both a horizontal and a vertical vial, this tool may be used on both planes. When setting up profiles and building walls, a plumb bob is also useful.

Drainage

Patios and decks built away from buildings will not normally require special drainage facilities. As soon as you build alongside a house, however, drainage becomes an important factor.

When paving or laying concrete floors adjacent to a house, the finished surface must be at least 150 mm (6 in) below the damp-proof course (DPC). Found in newer buildings, this is a plastic damp-proof membrane which is laid on the compacted fill before a concrete floor slab is cast, and is essential for controlling rising damp in buildings. The floor slab is usually 75-100 mm (3-4 in) thick, so you can easily assess its position in relation to the finished interior floor, even if it is not

visible on the outside. If there is no such membrane (as is the case in some older houses), it is still essential that the patio surface is below the internal floor level.

Where interior floors are made of timber, a patio should be about 150 mm (6 in) below the bottom of the floorboards. With decks there is more flexibility, and it may be possible to continue the slats at the same level. Nevertheless, when a deck is attached to a ledger, it is good practice to use flashing to prevent moisture from penetrating the space between the deck substructure and the wall. If crossbeams are simply attached to the house with joist hangers, this is not necessary.

In addition, rainwater must be channelled away from the building. You may need to build a gully or lay a precast concrete channel to carry the water, and it may be necessary to construct a soakaway or French drain filled with hardcore and stones. If you simply want to divert water which runs under the deck, a concrete gutter or drainage pipe will probably do the job. If the area beneath the deck is to be water-tight, you will need a solid floor surface (see page 63), and if you decide to build an overhead structure with a solid roof, guttering will be required. Usually, however, you simply need to ensure that the patio floor slopes away from the house by creating a gradient of about 1:40 (see page 19).

Although a deck may be raised above a slope, building a patio on a sloping site will mean excavating the soil and

redistributing it in order to provide a solid, stable surface for the paving. The most common method of levelling is to 'cut and fill'. This means removing soil from the top of the slope and filling in below to create a flat area. Take care, however, to compact the fill thoroughly, or the ground will not be stable.

If the soil under a deck is unstable, you may decide to build a retaining wall (see pages 72-73). When constructing a solid brick retaining wall, ensure that the space behind the wall is filled with compacted hardcore and stones, and leave weepholes at the base of the structure. It is wise to consult an engineer if retaining walls are to be higher than about 1.2 m (4 ft).

CONCRETE WORK

Basically a mixture of cement, sand, stone and water, concrete is a vital ingredient in all construction work. It forms the foundation for everything from walls and steps to the upright timbers of a deck.

Concrete is not difficult to make, although mixing by hand is hard work. However, some knowledge is necessary, and care should be taken to ensure that the correct quantities are used (see page 15). It must also be mixed properly.

Grades of concrete

Different mix proportions of cement, sand and stone result in different grades of concrete. The strength required will be determined by its function.

Low-strength concrete is used for most foundations and footings, and medium-strength concrete for reinforced footings, paths, steps and slabs. High-strength concrete is generally necessary for heavy-duty or industrial use only, or when there is a possibility of severe vibration. It is also suitable for driveways and carport floors.

Mixing

It is more practical to mix concrete in batches than to mix all you need at once. Use a strong, rigid container (a builder's bucket or large drum) to measure the materials by volume.

Hand mixing If you are mixing by hand, it is advisable to use a smaller-sized stone. Work on a clean, hard surface, or if that is not available, mix small quantities in a wheelbarrow to prevent the concrete from being contaminated by soil, and moisture being absorbed from the mixture.

Mix the sand and cement first to get a uniform colour. Then make a small crater in the centre and slowly add water, shovelling the sand and cement from the

You can use a wheelbarrow for mixing small amounts of concrete. Combine sand and cement, then add water, and lastly add crushed stone.

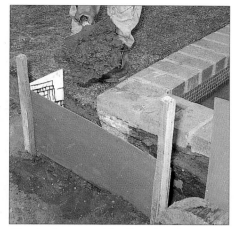

Wooden battens and hardboard used to make shuttering for containing wet concrete.

edges to the centre as you do so. When you have a soft, smooth mixture, spread the stone over it evenly and continue shovelling. If the concrete is too dry, add a little more water, but take care not to make it too runny.

Machine mixing When using a concrete mixer, load the stone first, together with a little water to clean the drum and prevent a build-up of mortar around the blades. Then load the sand, and finally the cement and water.

The materials required for one batch will depend on the size of the machine, which should never be loaded above its rated capacity. Always empty the drum completely before mixing a new batch, and wash it out thoroughly after use.

Formwork

While most foundations and footings are thrown below ground level, any *in situ* concrete cast above the ground will require shuttering or formwork to hold it in place while it sets.

Both wood and metal may be used to make formwork (metal is often formed specially for this purpose), although it must, of course, be strong and rigid enough to withstand the weight of the concrete so that the mixture cannot leak out.

Lay out the area to be concreted, as described on page 19. Before erecting the formwork, lightly oil any part that will be in contact with the concrete. It will then come away easily without damaging the structure when it is dismantled. Hold the formwork

in place with pegs, and nail pieces together if necessary. Using a spirit level, check that the top of the formwork is level, and insert wedges underneath to correct its position.

Laying the concrete

If water is absorbed from wet concrete, the concrete will weaken and may crack. To prevent this from happening, dampen the ground before pouring the concrete.

If you are casting a slab for a patio floor, you will need to form joints to prevent expansion and contraction from causing unsightly cracking. The simplest way to do this is by laying panels no larger than 3 m x 3 m (10 ft x 10 ft). Lay alternate panels one day, then the remaining panels on the next. The new concrete will abut the hardened panels, forming a natural joint.

When casting concrete in situ, *it is useful to nail lengths of wood to the straightedge to form handles. Two people can then compact the concrete by tamping it with a chopping movement.*

Levelling and smoothing concrete.

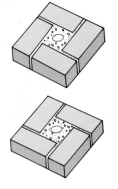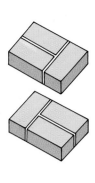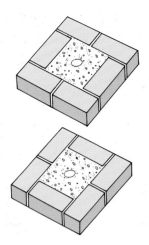

When building brick pillars, courses are laid in alternate directions so that they bond well.

Erect the formwork and cast each of the panels in a continuous operation. Pour the concrete until it is about 25 mm (1 in) above the level of the formwork, and compact it with a thick plank (fitted with handles at each end if you wish), using a chopping movement. When watery cement paste comes to the surface, use a sawing motion to level the concrete. If there are any gaps or hollows, fill these before smoothing the surface with a wooden float. To compact footings, use the back of a shovel instead of a plank.

If you want a rough, slip-proof patio surface, consider giving the concrete an exposed aggregate finish. Scatter 13.2 mm (½ in) stone over the wet surface and push the stones into the concrete with a wooden float. When the concrete has set (after about eight hours), brush the floor surface and spray it lightly with water.

Curing
Concrete hardens as a result of a chemical reaction between cement and water. If it is allowed to dry out too quickly, however, it will never gain its full strength, so it should always be cured or allowed to set over a few days.

Ideally, you should let it cure for at least 5 days, although some people leave it for only 24-48 hours. In cold weather, the surface should be covered with hessian or plastic to protect it from frost; otherwise simply sprinkle or spray with water from time to time to keep the concrete damp.

Colouring concrete
Both concrete and mortar (see above and page 95) may be coloured with powdered oxide pigments to achieve various shades of buff, ochre, brown, red, pink or green. This can be achieved by adding 5-15 kg of pigment to each cubic metre (8½-25 lb per cubic yard) of concrete or, if you are

colouring a screed or plaster, 8-25 kg to each cubic metre (14-42 lb per cubic yard) of mortar. Although you can usually get a fairly even finish using this method, you will need a lot of pigment. Alternatively, you can colour the surface: either sprinkle 150-250 g dry pigment per square metre (4-7 oz per square yard) straight onto the wet screed or plaster and work it in with a steel trowel, or mix it with cement and water, and brush onto the surface when dry (see page 71). Whichever way you apply it, surface colouring may result in a somewhat mottled effect.

BRICKLAYING AND PAVING
Bricklaying and paving are skills which are relatively easy to acquire, and one can achieve good results simply by ensuring that all bricks are laid square, level and plumb (see pages 19-20).

Mortar is essential for all bricklaying and for some methods of paving. A mixture of cement, sand, water and sometimes lime

A corner block in position.

(see page 15), it is mixed in exactly the same way as concrete (see pages 20-21). Mix only as much as you can use in two hours; as soon as it begins to stiffen, throw the mortar away. Never be tempted simply to add extra water to soften it, as this will weaken the mixture and probably cause it to become lumpy.

Bricklaying
Once you have mastered the technique of buttering and laying the bricks, you will be well equipped to tackle any garden brickwork. If you are inexperienced at this, practise using a bricklayer's trowel before you start work on a specific project.

Next, decide on the type of bond you will use (see page 23). The first course of bricks is laid on a concrete foundation (see pages 52-53), which must be clean and dry. Brush away any sand or debris and lay a strip of mortar on the surface. Use a trowel to form an uneven groove in the mortar and place the first brick on it. Push the brick gently but firmly and tap it with the trowel's wooden handle to level it. Butter the end of the second brick and slide it into position with the mortar against the first brick. While you work, use corner blocks and a builder's line to help you keep each row of bricks straight and even, and a gauge rod (see page 10) to ensure that all courses and mortar joints are exactly the same.

Place mortar on top of the first row of bricks, make a groove in it, then lay bricks as before. Use a spirit level on both vertical and horizontal surfaces, and a builder's square to check corners. If there are any gaps between the bricks, fill with mortar before laying the next course. Use a trowel to scrape any excess off the surface as you work. When laying facebricks, neaten the joints with a pointing tool or a piece of metal (see pages 11 and 88).

Examples of bonds used in bricklaying. From top: English bond, English garden wall bond, Flemish bond and stretcher bond.

When laying bricks, use a spirit level frequently to ensure that brickwork is level and plumb.

Bonds in brickwork It is essential to create a strong brick bond in the bricklaying process, since the wall will lack strength and stability if the load in it is not evenly distributed.

There are several different types of bond which may be used. The most common type internationally is stretcher bond, where each brick overlaps the one below by half. English bond is believed to be particularly strong, and is therefore popular for retaining walls. Here, courses of headers (bricks laid side-by-side) and stretchers are laid alternately. Other possibilities include English garden wall bond, which consists of a header course followed by three to five stretcher courses, and Flemish bond, with headers and stretchers in the same course.

Plastering or rendering Unless you are building with facebricks, you will have to plaster or render the surface. The plaster or render used for this is mixed in exactly the same way, and using the same ratio of cement and sand (see pages 13-15), as the mortar used for laying the bricks. To make the plaster or render more pliable and easier to apply, it is a good idea to use sand to which lime has been added. If you are adding lime yourself, use a cement:lime:sand ratio of 2:1:8.

Apply the mixture to the brickwork with a plasterer's trowel, pressing it down to ensure that it sticks to the surface. Cover the whole surface and leave for a short while before scraping with a screed board to flatten the plaster or render, and smoothing with a wooden float. If the weather is hot, sprinkle a little water on the plaster as you work. Neaten the corners with a corner trowel.

Plaster or render must be kept damp in the same way as concrete, to ensure that it cures and does not crack. Spray it lightly every now and then with a hosepipe; how often you need to do this will depend on the weather conditions.

Paving

Both rigid and flexible paving (see pages 24-25) have been laid for centuries. For instance, the ancient Romans laid small clay bricks on edge to form pavements and the floors of stables, while the Dutch have used flexible paving on reclaimed land so that it can be relaid as the ground settles. In Britain, clay paving has medieval origins.

Many types of material may be used to create a hard floor surface in the garden (see pages 12-13 and 48-50), but the basic methods used for laying them are the same. Paving must be laid so that it is flat and allows for proper drainage (see page 20), otherwise water and mud will accumulate. If flexible paving is laid over a water-tight sub-base, extra drainage will be necessary below the surface. In this case, open-jointed or perforated pipe may be laid at points where the water may settle below the paving, leading to a drain or soakaway.

Patterns and bonds There are various bonding patterns for rectangular pavers. The most common is probably running bond, which is similar to stretcher bond in a wall (see above). Basketweave, which may be laid either diagonally or at right angles to its edges, is also popular, as is stack bond, where bricks are laid in straight lines. The strongest bond is herringbone, which may also be laid diagonally or at right angles. Circular and curved patterns are only suitable if you are using the rigid paving method, as the joints will be irregular in shape.

Edge restraints Edging of some kind is always necessary when one is paving a patio, unless the patio is bounded by walls on all sides (see pages 52-53). There are many possibilities, ranging from bricks laid on edge, to concealed concrete and timber. Whatever style you choose, it must be securely placed in order for it to prevent the paving from moving.

A circular pattern in two colours adds interest to brick paving.

Slightly sloping bricks edge a paved area.

Stretcher bond.

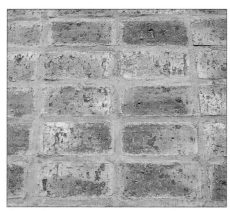

Stack bond.

Staggered basket weave.

Herringbone.

Flexible paving Probably the most popular method, flexible paving is cheaper and quicker to lay than other types. Bricks or blocks are laid on a bed of sand and the joints filled with extra sand. Mortar is required only for the edging (see page 23).

The sub-base of flexible paving must be stable, otherwise the paving can become displaced or collapse. When paving a patio, it is often sufficient to compact the ground thoroughly. If the ground is unstable, you will need to excavate and add a fairly substantial sub-base of crushed stone or gravel and compact it to about 150 mm (6 in). The sand on which the bricks are

laid should, ideally, be coarser than that used for jointing. The layer of sand should also be as thin as possible (30 mm, compacted to 25 mm; about 1 in) to accommodate fractionally different brick sizes, and should never be used to correct poor sub-base levels. A board may be used to level and compact the sand (see page 53).

Although some people recommend laying a sheet of plastic under the bedding sand when laying flexible paving, there is a school of thought that strongly opposes this practice on the grounds that it allows water to collect between the paving and induces moisture movement.

Paving bricks are laid in the chosen pattern as described in the step-by-step instructions on page 53. Do not make the mistake of allowing bricks or blocks to abut each other. This will considerably decrease the flexibility of the surface and may lead to undesirable movement of the pavers. Instead, aim for a narrow joint of 2-6 mm (⅛-¼ in). If the joint is too wide, the jointing sand, which is brushed into the joints, may blow away and the paving become destabilised. Use a rubber mallet to level the bricks or blocks and to straighten the lines of the joints. Hosing the newly paved surface lightly with water will help to consolidate the sand between the joints. As it settles, however, it may be necessary to sprinkle a little more sand on parts of the surface to fill any new gaps.

Rigid paving Although this is more time-consuming and costly than flexible paving, rigid paving is more durable and particularly useful when there are sudden changes in level. It is almost always used for steps and terraces, and is the obvious choice if there is an existing concrete base. Furthermore, it enables one to introduce curved and circular patterns which have irregularly shaped joints.

If you are laying paving on an old, uneven slab, you will need to screed the surface first. Use a 1:4 cement:sand mixture and aim for a 25 mm (1 in) layer. If you are casting new concrete, ensure that the sub-base is sound by compacting it and, if necessary, by bringing in stones or gravel to level it as previously described.

There are various ways of laying rigid paving, the preferred method being to place mortar on the screed and then butter the edge of each paver as you would for bricklaying. Joints should be about 10 mm (½ in) wide, and a 1:3 cement:sand mortar mix used. Alternatively, you can fill the joints later, or brush a dry cement-sand mix into them and then spray lightly with water. An advantage of

Bricks laid at an angle around a brick-paved patio.

Cutting bricks and pavers

There are several ways to cut a brick. You can use the sharp, chisel end of a brick hammer, or a bolster with a brick hammer or club hammer. Alternatively, if there is a lot of cutting to do, an angle grinder will be a more efficient tool.

When cutting bricks with a brick hammer, tap the brick with the chisel end to score a cutting line, and then give it a sharp blow along this line. Alternatively, place the brick on sand, score the surface of the brick, then hold the bolster firmly on this line and tap the handle firmly but gently with the club hammer. Either way, the brick should break neatly in two.

Using a chisel and brick hammer to cut a brick.

Cleaning and maintenance

Mortar that has dropped on the paving should, if possible, be removed straight away, although large lumps of mortar can be left to dry and be knocked off later with a wooden or plastic spatula. It should never be wiped off, as mortar smears will stain the paving. Instead, dab it with dry rags or newspaper to remove all water – this will make cleaning the paving easier. Once mortar has dried, it can be removed with spirits of salts. This substance contains hydrochloric acid and is highly poisonous,

Using an angle grinder to cut a brick.

so it is advisable to wear rubber gloves and gumboots when working with it. Dilute the liquid with lukewarm water in a ratio of about 1:20. Working over an area of not more than 2 m² (21 ft²) at a time, wet the paving so that the spirits of salts does not penetrate the joints, then splash the acid on with a bristle brush and leave it for a few minutes. Hose off the acid solution with lots of clean water.

Another common problem, especially when laying rigid paving, is that white salts sometimes crystallise on the surface as the paving dries out. There is little you can do about this except to let it weather naturally.

Paving around a salt-water swimming pool can also be problematic as the salt water can cause both clay and concrete paving bricks or blocks to deteriorate. You may be able to seal the pavers, but it will be wise to consult a specialist before paving the area.

In damp areas, a 10% solution of bleach or copper sulphate (which is available in some countries from swimming-pool or hardware shops) in water will usually kill any moss and algae that has grown.

filling the joints after laying the pavers is that an even joint can easily be achieved by using pieces of thin wood as spacers. However, the mortar may well stain the surface. Any mortar that is dropped on to the bricks should be removed immediately if possible, but do not wipe the surface.

Although edge restraints are not as vital as in flexible paving, they will prevent the bricks from becoming detached from the mortar bed. You will have to provide movement joints if the patio measures more than 6 m (20 ft) in either direction. Instead of mortar, fill joints with a suitable flexible material such as silicone rubber.

Hybrid method Many people prefer to use a hybrid method of paving. This involves laying bricks on sand and brushing in a weak mortar mix (either moist and crumbly or dry) between the joints; a cement:sand ratio of 1:6 is common for clay bricks, while 1:4 is recommended for concrete blocks and setts. The surface is then sprayed with water. The major disadvantage of the hybrid method is that weak joints often crack and this not only looks ugly, but can also cause the paving to move.

CARPENTRY

The carpentry skills required to build an attractive timber deck or pergola are not hard to master, and any DIY enthusiast should be able to tackle all of the projects in this book which involve woodwork. However, if your project is to be successful, you must always measure and cut the wood accurately. For this it helps to have the right tools for the job and to know how to use them. Recommended tools are listed on pages 10-12, and their uses are illustrated in several of the step-by-step projects.

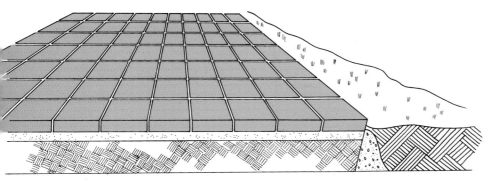

A strip of concrete, just below ground level, holds the paving in place.

Measuring

This may seem elementary, but it can be confusing when planning the position of multiple lengths of timber along a beam or other framework. The more accurate your measuring, the easier it will be to erect a structure, however simple.

When positioning crosspieces on a beam or ledger, the best way to ensure that the spacing of the timbers is regular is to determine where the midpoint of the width of each piece should lie, rather than trying to estimate the spaces between the pieces. So, for example, if 44 mm thick (1¾ in) joists must be positioned on a beam at 500 mm (1 ft 7½ in) centres, measure points 500 mm (1 ft 7½ in) apart and attach the centre of each joist at these points. However, the spaces between the timbers will be 456 mm (1 ft 5¾ in) wide.

Drilling a pilot hole for a cuphead (coach) bolt.

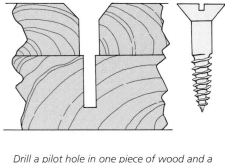

Drill a pilot hole in one piece of wood and a thicker clearance hole in the other, about the same size as the screw shank.

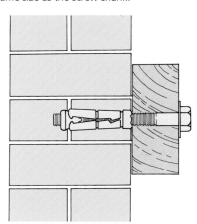

The materials used to build your house will largely determine which connectors are used to secure a ledger or other timber in position. A coach bolt may be used for a timber-frame house (left) and an expansion (Rawl) bolt to attach the wood to masonry (right).

Always use the correct drill bit for the job.

Cutting

Normally you will cut wood across the grain. If you are using a handsaw, you will find it easier to make a perfectly vertical, square cut if you have clamped the wood on to a workbench. Alternatively, screw a straight-edged piece of wood to the edge of your workbench or other flat surface, and push the length of timber you are sawing up against it to keep it in position.

An even better option, which will produce a straighter, more accurate cut, is to use a circular saw. Furthermore, when an angled cut is required, to mitre corners for instances, this power tool may simply be adjusted to achieve the desired angle. When measuring wood, bear in mind that a power saw will shave off a little extra wood during the cutting process.

Whatever the angle, it is essential to ensure a clean finish. Never force the saw through the wood – if it does not cut easily, it is probably blunt. You should be able to smooth the end with a piece of sandpaper.

Connecting

There are many connectors on the market for fastening timbers to each other and to other materials, and wood joints can be made in different ways.

Fasteners Wood can be joined with a variety of nails, screws and bolts (see page 17-18). It is good practice to screw thinner pieces of wood to thicker ones; to ensure a strong join, use a screw long enough to go through both pieces of wood, or about three times as long as the thickness of the top piece if the timbers are unequal in thickness. When screwing or bolting two pieces together, drill a pilot hole slightly shorter than the length and smaller than the diameter of the fastener, unless you are using small screws in softer woods, in which case a bradawl is all you will need. For screws with countersunk heads, you will also need a countersink drill bit. Twist the screw so that the head is below the surface of the wood and cover it with wood filler, epoxy or a wood plug.

It is also advisable to drill a pilot hole before nailing, when working with a very

hard wood. This will make your job much easier and will prevent the timber from splitting. Again, the hole should be smaller than the nail, or the nail will not grip the timber. Blunt the tips of nails when working with soft wood; this will also help to prevent splitting. When hammering, take care not to 'bruise' or dent the wood. Use a pointed nail punch (or nail set) to drive the nail right into the wood. If you do bruise the timber, sponge it with hot water which will cause it to swell and help repair the damage.

You can either fill over a nail, or, if you want to hide it completely, use a chisel to prise up a sliver of wood before nailing, and glue it back into place afterwards.

When you cannot get to the end of the wood (if two joists abut a beam in line with each other, for instance), skew-nail or skew-screw the wood together. This means driving in a screw or nail at an angle so that it penetrates the adjacent piece of wood.

Coach screws and hexagonal bolts may be tightened with a spanner. To secure cuphead bolts (coach bolts), first hammer them into place, then use a shifting spanner to fasten the nut.

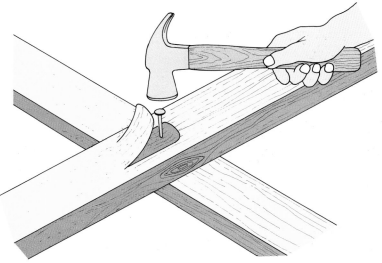

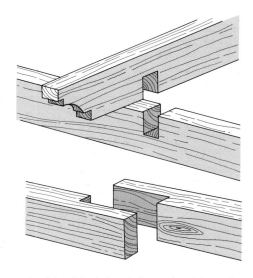

Hide a nail by prising up a sliver of wood, then covering the head of the nail with it once you have knocked the nail into place.

Lap joints join timbers in line and at right angles.

Joints There is no need for elaborate joints in outdoor structures. They must just look neat and be strong enough to secure the timber without there being any possibility of the structure collapsing.

Most of the time you can rely on ordinary butt joints which are formed simply by nailing, screwing or bolting timbers together, and which do not require any complex carpentry skills. In some cases, two pieces of wood may overlap each other to form a T- or cross-butt joint. A railing post, for instance, may be positioned against the substructure of the deck and bolted into place, and bracing (see page 35) will overlap the posts themselves. Make sure that the wood is properly cut (see page 26) otherwise the joint will not be absolutely flush. To strengthen the joint, you can apply a waterproof wood glue before fastening.

A lap joint is particularly useful when constructing railings around a deck.

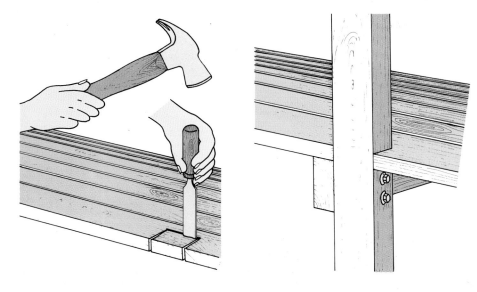

It may be necessary to notch decking to accommodate posts for railings. The sides can be cut with a handsaw, but you will need a chisel to cut the back of the notch.

Wooden reinforcing blocks or metal angle brackets may be used to strengthen the corners if necessary. These are screwed into place on either the inside or the outside of a corner, depending on what you are building.

A lap joint (see illustrations) is a little more complicated. Equal chunks of wood are cut out of two lengths of timber so that the lengths slot together forming a neat, well-bonded joint. A lap joint can be made at virtually any angle, and is particularly useful when joining the diagonal slats of railings (see pages 44-45), or when joining two lengths of timber end on.

Notching (see illustrations) is often useful when building decking, especially when fitting handrails and railings. You can usually notch timber with a chisel and handsaw, although accuracy is important. If the space you provide for a post is too large, the post will not fit snugly.

DECKS

The most obvious reasons for building a deck are to add living space to a house and to utilise steeply sloping ground which might otherwise be hard to manage. There are other benefits too, ranging from improving the look of your garden and providing a low-maintenance surface, to increasing the value of your property.

FUNCTION

Whether it is an extension of your house or freestanding, a deck is a particularly useful option where rocky ground cannot be flattened easily, or where the ground becomes mushy or waterlogged during heavy rains.

Attached to a house, a deck will visually enlarge the interior, especially where the floor surface is a continuation of the indoor flooring. Such a deck is often constructed as an alternative to the more conventional verandah or porch, and is particularly suitable if the house is situated on a slope. Furthermore, if the deck is built some distance from the ground, it could also enable you to capture a view which would otherwise be missed.

In the garden, a multilevel timber deck will introduce the concept of terracing without requiring expensive excavations, and will be a distinctive feature in your garden. Timber decking can also be erected around a swimming pool, hot tub or other garden feature.

Your deck's usefulness will be increased if you include additional features in the design. Built-in working surfaces, seats and storage will make entertaining much easier and more pleasurable, while a hot-water spa or a swimming pool will encourage you to make use of the area more frequently. A simple pergola or overhead could be an attractive feature; if creepers are trained over it or roofing material is installed, the pergola will provide shade and (depending on the roofing material chosen) protect the area from the elements.

Other practical details must not be overlooked: steps or ramps will be necessary if you wish to link your deck with ground level and other adjoining surfaces; for safety reasons, railings must be included if your deck or patio is raised; while screens will increase privacy and shield the deck in windy weather.

Finally, finishing touches, including plants and lighting, must be considered.

Karri was used for the slats of this covered deck; the rest of the structure was made from Oregon pine.

DESIGN AND STYLE

Using existing architecture and garden style as a guide, ensure that your deck is in proportion with the property as a whole, as well as with other garden features and the house.

If you have the space, consider erecting multilevel decking or introducing interesting angles instead of putting up a rectangular platform. Give thought to the style of the actual framework – the footings and posts, beams, joists and ledgers (see page 34). You may have to brace some of the timber (depending on the size of the deck and the height of the posts), but bracing too can be both decorative and functional. You may decide to support the decking on brick pillars rather than wooden posts.

The maximum possible height of a post, the distance which can be bridged by a piece of timber, and the spacing of structural timbers will depend on many factors, including the kind of wood you are using and the dimensions of its cross-section. When you have decided on the overall size of the structure, you will need to determine the cross-sections and spans of the beams – a timber supplier or your local authority should have tables containing the necessary information.

Once you have chosen a basic design, you can experiment on paper with floor surface patterns and railings. Just like paving, wood can be laid in a variety of patterns; if you want a more complex pattern than conventional plank flooring, you may like to use a chequerboard or herringbone design for interest. These involve more cutting, and you will also have to ensure that the ends of each piece of decking are supported.

Railings are usually included for safety reasons, but they can also enhance the appearance of the deck. There are many options, from vertical or horizontal rails to criss-crossed slats or intricate latticework.

TYPES

Low-level decks

A low-level deck can be built as a freestanding structure in the garden (see project on pages 38-40) or attached to the house – it may effectively be a timber patio in some cases. It is probably also the only type of deck which you may be able to construct without submitting plans.

Even though timber decking is generally more expensive than paving, building a low-level deck could prove to be more cost-effective than excavating in a garden which is uneven and rocky underfoot. Furthermore, you will be creating a level surface for outdoor activities.

Attached decks

As a deck is a relatively simple way of extending one's living space, one of the most common deck types is that which is attached to the house.

To secure the wooden framework to the house, basic construction methods are used. A ledger is attached to the outside wall using the appropriate fasteners (see pages 26 and 34). Coach screws may be used if you have a timber-frame house, or Rawl bolts with bricks and mortar. The ledger must line up with the rest of the beams – together the ledgers and beams support the joists, which in turn support the decking slats; if levels are not accurate, the decking will slope or wobble. Because the deck abuts the house, you must take particular care to prevent water from pooling on or underneath the structure, or seeping into the house (see page 20).

Multilevel decks

A multilevel deck can be a wonderful landscaping tool, providing access to the house while forming terraces in the garden.

An obvious way to construct a multilevel deck is to vary the height of the posts. You will probably need to build steps or a staircase to move between levels, but if there is not much difference in height between the two levels, one can usually rest the joists for the upper level on top of a beam. The adjacent lower level can then be supported on joist hangers attached to the side of the same beam. The visual effect of multilevel decking is enhanced if the direction of the decking slats is changed between levels.

Swimming pool or spa deck

A deck which surrounds a pool or spa, or is constructed alongside one, can be an attractive addition to your outdoor area. These decks are particularly useful when a pool has been built into a slope, as they enable one to extend the poolside area.

A beautifully weathered timber deck surrounds a spa flowing into a two-tiered swimming pool.

Decking slats have been used around the spa, as well as to construct steps leading to a deck.

Multilevel decking effectively used as a landscaping tool.

Angles are used to create an interesting effect on this poolside deck.

A hot-water spa set in a compact deck with a magnificent view.

In the case of a spa or hot tub, the deck can be as big or as small as you wish. It may also be built so that the top of the spa is on the same level as the deck; this will usually mean sinking the spa into the ground. If it is installed above ground, as hot tubs usually are, the completed deck floor may be below the surface of the water, and the outsides of the hot tub encased in timber.

Since hot tubs and some spas are circular, a jigsaw will be invaluable for cutting the decking to fit its shape.

Angled decks

A deck does not have to be regular in shape. Interesting angles may add character and charm to a small deck, and could enable you to take advantage of unused corners of the garden. Cutting the corners of stepped rectangular areas may also soften the effect of these more regular forms. Although basic construction follows the same procedure, there will inevitably be more cutting (see page 26) and, if you are not careful, greater wastage.

Japanese-style decks

While it is possible to introduce a Japanese theme with decking anywhere in the garden, the traditional Japanese *engawa* is a deck which wraps around the house. Furthermore, it extends the interior floor surface outside, creating a single-level, indoor-outdoor platform which may be divided by sliding doors or *shojis* (rice paper screens).

This type of deck is typically built one step above ground level, with the decking slats laid parallel to the house, and is used to display containers, sculptures or other works of art.

The *engawa* is built in the same way as other decks, although it is often more practical to set the crossbeams on short brick piers rather than posts. Since the *engawa* is attached to the house, it is also necessary to secure a ledger along the foundation wall to support the decking slats. A fascia runs across the ends of the beams to ground level, thus hiding the substructure of the deck.

Cantilevered decks

More exacting to design and to construct, cantilevering is the ideal solution for a deck which will extend over water. It may also be an attractive option for a deck built on the upper level of a double- or triple-storey house.

Instead of resting directly on posts or columns, a cantilevered deck rests on horizontal or angled supports such as heavy wooden beams or concealed,

Decking has been used for a compact jetty as well as for a second-floor verandah.

reinforced-steel girders. These are built into the wall to which the deck is attached, so that the deck is supported from the side only.

An accomplished handyman may be able to construct a small deck of this nature, but if you do not have the experience, use another method or call in a professional designer and builder.

If you are building a house and like the idea of a cantilevered deck, you can often extend floor beams, including the outside area in the design of the building itself.

Jetties and bridges

Decking principles are frequently used for jetties and bridges where a stream runs through the garden or where there is a substantial water feature.

The most important factor here is secure anchorage in the water. In most cases it will be necessary to consult a structural engineer when you design the foundations of the structure. Piling will be required, and this should always be professionally designed and installed. Unless you have considerable building experience, jetties and bridges are not recommended as DIY projects. Rather consult the experts, or at least get professional help to do the piling, then finish off the decking yourself.

A small cantilevered deck leads from a second-storey doorway.

A deck attached to a house on a steep property effectively extends the living space.

Decking over steep slopes

When constructing a deck over a steep slope, it is advisable to consult an engineer to ensure that the posts are adequately anchored. In some instances this might involve drilling into rock and additional professional assistance may be required.

For major structures it is necessary to bore into the ground and pour substantial concrete pile foundations, which should be well reinforced to form a strong base. Consequently, they should always be designed by and constructed under the supervision of a qualified engineer.

SURFACE MATERIALS

The most popular material for decks throughout the world is undoubtedly timber. Although it is commonly used on its own, timber can also be combined with other materials, for instance if the deck leads to a brick-paved or tiled patio. However, there are some instances when a concrete slab could be preferable. Concrete decks are often cantilevered, and may be topped with a variety of materials.

Timber

There are several advantages to using timber for decks – apart from its attractive finish, it is also reasonably affordable,

lightweight and easy to work with. Although your choice of wood may be somewhat limited by what is available in your area, various types are suitable. The following are the most durable: afrormosia, an attractive yellow-brown species from West Africa; balau, a fine-textured wood noted for its strength and durability in hot, humid climates; beech, which is straight-grained and pale in colour; Californian redwood, valued for its resistance to decay and infestation; Western red cedar and the pinkish cerejeira, both of which are particularly easy to work with; oak (especially American red and American white), which is attractive, strong and versatile; Philippine mahogany, a durable timber that varies in colour from light to dark red; meranti, a versatile Malaysian wood; and teak which, although expensive, is one of the best timbers available for decks and furniture alike.

The decks built for the projects in this book were made from karri, a type of eucalyptus originating in Australia. It is similar in appearance to jarrah, another kind of eucalyptus, but much stronger. Although karri is difficult to cut with hand tools and has to be predrilled when nailing, its strength is an advantage when it comes to building decks.

Concrete

Concrete decking, whether supported on pillars or cantilevered, is almost always built at the same time as the rest of the house, rather than as an extension to be added on later. In some cases, it is nevertheless a more viable option than wooden decking, in particular when a watertight surface is essential, such as above a garage or a ground-floor room.

The concrete may be cast *in situ*, using formwork, or alternatively, precast, pre-stressed slabs may be used. The latter are extremely heavy and are usually erected by the manufacturers. Whichever option you choose, you will probably want to top the concrete surface with tiles, brick pavers, reconstituted stone, or some other attractive material, as you would a patio (see pages 63-65).

ALTERNATIVE METHODS OF CONSTRUCTION

The basic method of deck construction involves erecting a wooden framework of beams and joists which are suspended on top of posts. Certain conditions, such as a very steep site, water, or rocky, unstable or marshy soil, will call for special techniques and materials – reinforced concrete, steel and so on.

Anatomy of a split-level deck attached to a house by means of a ledger. Blocking between the joists prevents them from buckling, and posts are anchored to foundation footings for stability. A section of the deck has been specially designed to fit around a tree.

Upright supports

All decks, except those which are cantilevered, require piers or posts to keep the timber level and above the ground.

Posts and poles Suitable timber dimensions are usually specified by local authorities, as structural timbers must be able to carry the load of the deck above. The spacing of uprights will also be governed by local regulations, and will depend partly on the type of wood used – some kinds can span longer distances than others. If in doubt, seek the advice of a timber merchant.

When planed wood is used, blocks are often sandwiched between two lengths of timber for strength and stability (see pages 35 and 43). The blocks, or spacers, must be the same width as the beams, as these are also fixed between the timbers.

While it is possible to sink the upright timber supports into the ground and bed them in concrete, it is more usual to set post anchors into concrete footings or piers, then bolt the posts to them.

There are various types of post anchor on the market; alternatively you can have them specially made by an engineering firm. Whatever the design, it is usually preferable to allow a slight gap between the concrete and the wood; this prevents excess water from rotting the post.

The structure of this deck can be clearly seen from beneath. One beam is attached to the wall to create a ledger on which the joists rest, and the other is supported on a brick pillar.

Concrete columns When a deck is constructed on a particularly steep slope, reinforced concrete columns sometimes replace the more usual timber uprights. The simplest way of constructing these is to use cylindrical forms into which the concrete is poured. However, if you are building the deck yourself, it is advisable not to make concrete columns any higher than about a metre (3 ft).

Beams have been built into plastered brick pillars, and spacers used in a practical, visually pleasing way.

Steel posts In some instances, steel posts may be required. Like substantial concrete columns, however, these will have to be specified by an engineer, and the structure should be professionally installed.

Brick piers Another possible option, and one which appeals to many do-it-yourselfers, is to construct brick piers instead of timber posts. Beams are then supported on the piers in much the same way as overhead timbers are attached to pergola uprights (see page 85), or they could be built into the brickwork.

Beams are bolted to brick piers.

Timber connections

Various screws and bolts are used to connect pieces of wood to each other (see pages 17-18), but the actual methods of connection can vary.

Uprights The type of upright used to construct the deck will determine, to a large extent, the method of connection chosen. If you have built a brick pier, you could bolt a post-beam connector to the top to support the beam. Alternatively, you could secure the beams with strapping, as illustrated on page 85. When building with poles, you will usually have to use connectors.

Sawn and planed timber uprights can be bolted to the beams in the same way as poles are. Where spacer blocks are sandwiched between two upright timbers, the beam will be slotted in above the block of wood and secured with cuphead bolts.

If thicker, single pieces of timber are used as uprights, the beams are often secured to them with angle brackets or special T-straps. Alternatively, a double beam may be used, with the single upright sandwiched between the two beams.

Ledgers The step-by-step instructions for the Pool Deck on pages 41-45 illustrate how to attach a ledger to a beam. Joists are then screwed to the ledgers or beams, either straight through the beam or by skew-screwing (see page 44).

Where a ledger is fixed to the wall, it is positioned so that its top is level with the top of the ledger attached to the opposite beam. This is vital to ensure that the joists – and therefore the decking slats – are absolutely level and even. Use a spirit level to check that each ledger is horizontal, and a line or water level to ensure that the tops of the ledgers are all at exactly the same height as each other.

If there is no roofing material covering the deck, it is wise to fit galvanised flashing over the ledger to prevent moisture from damaging the wood. Available in a roll, the flashing is positioned along the wall and over the top of the ledger to cover the join between the two, and is nailed on to the wood.

Joists and beams Instead of attaching a ledger, you could use joist hangers. These often appeal to the DIY deck-builder as they create foolproof butt joints (see page 27) between joists and load-bearing beams. You may, however, find this method more costly and time consuming, as each joist hanger will have to be screwed or bolted into place.

When joists are attached to a wall with joist hangers, they are secured in exactly the same way as a pergola beam would be (see pages 84-85). If your deck design has unusual angles or you are creating decking patterns (see page 36), angled joist hangers are particularly useful. They enable you to connect the timber without having to cut the ends to the required angle.

Where a joist rests on a concrete slab, an angle bracket is the obvious connector to use (see page 44). It is bolted to the concrete surface and the wood secured to the other side of the bracket.

For a small, simple deck structure, you can bolt joists to the face of the beam with joist hangers or ledgers.

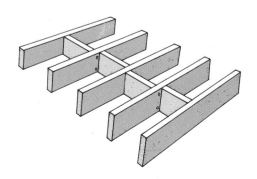

Staggered blocking prevents joists from twisting or moving.

Blocking and bracing It may be necessary to bridge joists to prevent them from twisting, buckling and moving, and to help stabilise the structure. Spacers the same thickness as the joists may be used for staggered blocking, while thinner battens may be used for cross-bracing (see page 85). Both are simply nailed into position during construction. If the joists are supported at least every 2.5 m (8 ft), blocking will not be necessary.

In some instances, posts may also have to be braced to prevent lateral movement. Whether you erect bracing will usually depend on the height of the post and the size of the deck. While local authorities will have their own set of specifications, a good rule of thumb is to brace the upright timbers of any deck which is wider than 6 m (20 ft), taller than 3.6 m (12 ft) if it is attached to a wall, or taller than 1 m (3 ft) if it is totally freestanding. It is also wise to brace the posts if the structure is likely to be exposed to high winds.

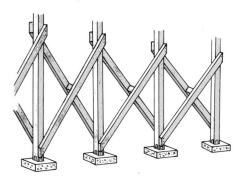

X-bracing with block spacers.

The method of bracing will depend on the design of your deck, but possibilities include X-bracing, which is attached diagonally, W-bracing, which omits one of each pair of the crosspieces used for X-bracing and extends across several uprights, and Y-bracing, which is always installed at the top of the posts.

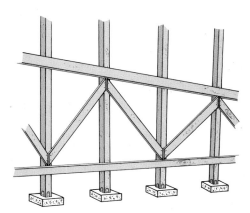

W-bracing spans several posts.

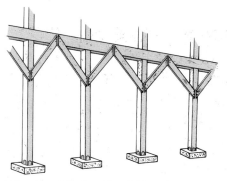

Y-bracing at the top of upright posts.

Decking slats These may be either nailed or screwed to the joists (both methods are illustrated on pages 40 and 44). Although brass, anodised or stainless-steel connectors should be used to prevent rust stains, you may like to plug the holes with pieces of wood.

When creating patterns with the wood, remember that, besides each piece of wood resting on joists along its length, the ends of every piece must be supported too. The more complicated the pattern you create, therefore, the more elaborate the deck's substructure will have to be.

Fascia boards To neaten the sides of the deck, a fascia or broad rim joist is usually nailed or screwed to the beams. Where two boards meet at a corner, the ends of the timber must be mitre-cut at a 45° angle.

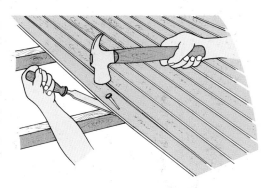

If decking slats are slightly warped, straighten them with a wood chisel and hammer; prise the slats apart very gently to avoid damaging them.

Fascia boards neaten the sides of an attractive deck attached to the side of a house.

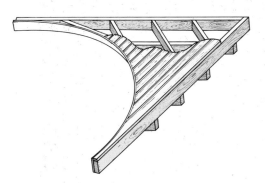

When building a deck around a hot-water spa, allow the slats to overlap the sub-structure, and neaten with a thin cover strip which will bend to fit the curve.

An attractive wooden railing around a deck built on a steep slope.

Weathered varnish is stripped before the timber can be recoated.

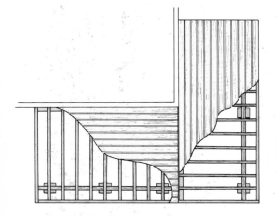

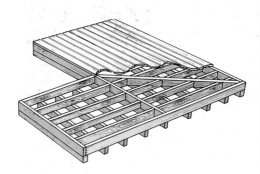

It is easy to change the surface pattern of decking slats when the structure turns a corner.

Railings Most decks have railings of some kind. There are numerous design possiblities, some of which are discussed on page 28. Safety factors often determine the height and spacing of the railings. Your local authority will advise.

Railing posts are usually bolted to the substructure of the deck (joists or beams), and supporting rails are secured *in situ*. A variety of connectors may be used – for examples, see page 18.

Maintenance

It is vital to maintain all parts of a deck. If paint or varnish starts peeling or flaking, sand the affected timber and recoat it before the wood begins to deteriorate. If you leave it, you may have to strip the entire surface before recoating. In the case of any timbers splitting or rotting, replace them immediately to avoid expensive structural repairs at a later stage.

The old decking has been removed and the beams coated with bitumen before new slats are fitted.

A simple, rustic deck made with poles and wide, sawn-timber slats.

LOW-LEVEL GARDEN DECK

This simple platform deck is an ideal project for anybody with basic carpentry skills. Because it is a small, low-level deck, the framework can be bolted together before the posts are concreted into the ground. Although there was only a very slight gradient in this garden, the design could also be constructed alongside a house built on a flat plot, or adapted for a more steeply sloping site.

STEP 5

to the beams at these points (directly over the join if you have used two pieces of wood to form the longer beam).

Materials
For a 5 m x 3 m (16 ft 5 in x 10 ft) deck:
2 x 5 m x 144 mm x 44 mm (16 ft 5 in x 5½ in x 1¾ in) beams
3 x 3 m x 144 mm x 44 mm (10 ft x 5½ in x 1¾ in) beams
10 x 2.5 m x 144 mm x 44 mm (8 ft 2½ in x 5½ in x 1¾ in) joists
6 x 360-600 mm (1 ft 2 in-2 ft) offcuts of wood
8 or more 144 mm x 44 mm (5½ in x 1¾ in) posts
50 x 3 m x 96 mm x 22 mm (10 ft x 3¾ in x ⅞ in) decking slats
72 x 6 mm x 70 mm (¼ in x 2¾ in) anodised self-tapping screws
20 x 10 mm x 90 mm (⅜ in x 3½ in) cuphead bolts with nuts and washers
700 x 50 mm (2 in) stainless-steel nails
50 kg (110 lb) cement
200 kg (440 lb) sand
200 kg (440 lb) stone

Preparation
1. Wood that is longer than required will have to be cut to size; some cutting can be done before work begins on assembling the deck, but be careful as you will need to double-check some of the measurements for accuracy during construction. If you cannot get 5 m (16 ft 5 in) lengths of wood for the framework, buy shorter pieces and join them together, as shown in Step 5.

2. For a professional finish, bevel the top edges of the decking slats with a router (or order planed wood with 45° bevelled edges).

3. Sand all the timber and give it one coat of sealer before you begin building. This is particularly important for sections

of wood which will abut other pieces or which will be inaccessible once the structure is complete.

Constructing the framework
4. Using an electric drill attachment and three anodised self-tapping screws at each connecting point, drill and screw the two 5 m (16 ft 5 in) lengths to the ends of one of the 3 m (10 ft) pieces of wood.

STEP 4

5. If you are joining two shorter pieces of wood to form each of the longer sides of the deck, cut away a block of wood 100 mm (4 in) long and half the width of the beam (22 mm or ⅞ in) from one end of both pieces of timber, so that they slot together to form a lap joint. Holding the two pieces together in position, drill four equally spaced holes where they join. Secure each join with four cuphead bolts.

6. Measure the central point along each of the 5 m (16 ft 5 in) beams and mark with a pencil. Following the instructions given in step 4, connect the central crosspiece

STEP 6

7. Attach the third 3 m (10 ft) length at the open end of the framework.

8. The joists should be a little less than 2.5 m (8 ft 3 in) long. It is essential, however, to check the distances between the crosspieces before cutting. Since timber frequently bows (particularly in the centre of an unsupported span), the measurements at either end will be the most accurate.

STEP 8

9. Mark a cutting line on all ten pieces of timber, using a builder's square for accuracy. If the joist timbers are longer than required, the offcuts will be suitable for the short posts.

STEP 9

10. Cut off the ends with a circular saw. If you are not working with a very hard wood, you may be able to use a handsaw instead. If the ends of the timber have been rough-cut (which is usually the case), it is unlikely that they will be exactly square. Trim both ends, making sure that your measurements are correct.

STEP 10

11. It is essential that the ends of the joists are sealed (see pages 16-17) before securing them to the beams with anodised screws.

12. If you take the easy option and screw both sets of joists to the central crosspiece, they will not run in a completely straight

STEP 11

line. This is not critical, except that the nails which secure the decking pieces will not be quite in line. If you wish to align the joists, however, skew-nail the end of one of each pair of joists. Whichever method you use, space the timber at 500 mm (1 ft 7½ in) centres, and check with a spirit level to ensure that they are all level.

13. If the timber bows excessively, you may have to clamp some of the wood in position before screwing it down.

14. Using a combination square, check all timber joins to make absolutely certain that they are at right angles.

STEP 14

Levelling the framework
15. Before you position the posts and concrete them into the ground, you must get the completed framework level. Do this by stacking offcuts under the central beam and by screwing about six short lengths to the inside edges (in the photograph, these are the upright

STEP 15

pieces which you see extending above the top of the framework). Use a spirit level to ensure accuracy.

Positioning the posts
16. For the structure to be stable, it will need to be supported on at least eight permanent posts. To strengthen the deck and stop any sideways movement, position posts on the joins and as close to the outer corners of the deck as possible.

STEP 16

STEP 20

STEP 21

17. Dig 300 mm x 300 mm x 300 mm (12 in x 12 in x 12 in) holes for the post footings.

18. Bolt the posts to the framework, ensuring that the tops of the posts are flush with the joists. Note that you can utilise the bolts which are already in place at the joins by unfastening and rebolting them.

19. Now mix cement, sand and stone in the ratio 1:4:4 and pour the concrete into the holes dug for the foundation footings. Allow to set thoroughly for 24-48 hours before removing the temporary supports.

21. Nail the slats to the joists, using a 5 mm (¼ in) spacer to space the slats accurately. If you are working with very hard wood, you will have to drill holes for the nails. This is easily done with a fine drill bit.

22. If you wish, you can close the open sides of the deck with additional slats.

Finishing
23. Fill the holes with epoxy or a powder filler mixed with a little sawdust; allow to dry and then sand so that the finished surface is even.

24. Cut uneven edges with a jigsaw, sand, and finally seal or varnish the entire deck.

STEP 19

Attaching the decking
20. Position the slats on the joists, working with about six boards at a time. Use a chalk line to ensure that the nails will be hammered in in a straight line along the joists.

The completed low-level deck is a perfect place for weekend entertaining.

POOL DECK

This wooden deck alongside a swimming pool is more complicated than the Low-level Deck, but still well within the capabilities of competent do-it-yourselfers. Since no two sites are the same, you will have to adapt the dimensions and height of the posts to suit your garden. The deck illustrated for this project has only seven supporting posts; the ends of two of the beams are supported on concrete. Although the procedure for resting a beam on concrete is shown, materials are quantified for a deck in which all the beams are supported on post anchors. The railing extends fully along three sides, and quantities of materials are calculated accordingly. If you wish to construct the deck so that it adjoins the house, only six post anchors will be required, but you will need to install a ledger against the wall (see page 34).

STEP 1

Preparation

1. The preparation of the timber is the same as for the Low-level Deck. Although you can precut most of the timber, remember that once you start working, there will inevitably be minor changes and it is wise to check all dimensions *in situ*. Any wood that will be inaccessible once the deck is assembled must be sealed before the timbers are secured.

2. If you are constructing a deck in a sloping garden, you may have to remove some soil from the site. In many instances you will be able to do this once the posts are in position. The slope here was unstable, so a retaining wall, made of precast blocks, was built before the deck was completed (see pages 72-74).

STEP 3

Setting out

3. Set out the site using pegs and string, so that the string extends beyond the corners of the planned structure by at least 500 mm (1 ft 8 in). This will help you to ensure that the structure is square.

4. Use a builder's square to check that the corners are at right angles and a line level to ensure that the string is horizontal. The 3:4:5 method (see page 19) will enable

Materials

For a 5 m x 6 m (16 ft 5 in x 19 ft 8 in) deck:
60 kg (130 lb) cement
225 kg (500 lb) sand
225 kg (500 lb) stone
9 x 144 mm x 44 mm (5½ in x 1¾ in) posts, lengths as appropriate
9 or more 150 mm x 144 mm x 44 mm (6 in x 5½ in x 1¾ in) timber spacer blocks
3 x 6 m x 144 mm x 44 mm (19 ft 8 in x 5½ in x 1¾ in) beams
22 x 2.5 m x 144 mm x 44 mm (8 ft 2½ in x 5½ in x 1¾ in) joists
8 x 2.5 m x 69 mm x 44 mm (8 ft 2½ in x 2¾ in x 1¾ in) ledgers
49 x 4.8 m x 96 mm x 22 mm (15 ft 9 in x 3¾ in x ⅞ in) decking slats
49 x 1.2 m x 96 mm x 22 mm (3 ft 11 in x 3¾ in x ⅞ in) decking slats
2 x 5 m x 220 mm x 32 mm (16 ft 5 in x 8½ in x 1¼ in) fascia boards, or sufficient wood to join
9 post anchors
42 x 150 mm (6 in) cuphead bolts with nuts and washers
2 x 150 mm (6 in) cuphead bolts with nuts and washers for each spacer block

48 x 13 mm x 70 mm (½ in x 2¾ in) hexagonal bolts with nuts and washers
97 x 6 mm x 70 mm (¼ in x 2¾ in) anodised self-tapping screws
1,078 x 6 mm x 40 mm (¼ in x 1½ in) anodised self-tapping screws

For the railing:
16 x 920 mm x 69 mm x 69 mm (3 ft x 2¾ in x 2¾ in) posts
32 x 1.5 m x 69 mm x 44 mm (5 ft x 2¾ in x 1¾ in) crosspieces
8 x 2.5 m x 96 mm x 22 mm (8 ft 2½ in x 3¾ in x ⅞ in) timber railings
4 x 3 m x 96 mm x 22 mm (9 ft 10 in x 3¾ in x ⅞ in) timber railings
4 x 2.5 m x 106 mm x 32 mm (8 ft 2½ in x 4 in x 1¼ in) timber cappings
2 x 3 m x 106 mm x 32 mm (9 ft 10 in x 4 in x 1¼ in) timber cappings
32 x 90 mm (3½ in) cuphead bolts with nuts and washers
128 x 8 mm x 40 mm (⅜ in x 1½ in) anodised self-tapping screws
96 x 8 mm x 70 mm (⅜ in x 2¾ in) anodised self-tapping screws

STEP 4

you to cross-check all measurements and make absolutely sure that the lines are perpendicular.

Foundations
5. Dig nine 300 mm x 300 mm x 300 mm (12 in x 12 in x 12 in) footings for the post anchors. These will determine the position of the posts which will support the substructure of the deck, and they should therefore be equally spaced.

STEP 6

6. Mix concrete in the ratio 1:4:4 and half-fill one of the holes. Position a post anchor in the concrete.

7. Use a spirit level to make sure that the base is level and plumb before filling the hole with more concrete.

STEP 7

STEP 9

8. Repeat steps 6 and 7 for the eight remaining holes.

9. String a line between the post anchors to check that each row of posts will be straight.

Preparing the beams
10. If any of the beams are to rest on concrete, it is vital to use bitumen where the two surfaces meet. This will help to prevent wood rot which can so easily occur if the timber is constantly wet. Use a paint brush to coat the two surfaces thoroughly.

STEP 10

11. If you are setting any of the beams on concrete (see pages 21-22 for instructions on casting concrete *in situ*), cut a piece out of the end of the beam and place the beam on the concrete. Use a spirit level to ensure that the beam is level, and secure it with angle brackets and coach screws (see step 25). Note that in this instance, the beam is to be positioned so that it is level with any adjacent hard surface – in this case, a brick coping around the swimming pool.

STEP 12

Positioning the posts

12. Set the posts in place. Get someone to hold them upright, or clamp them while you drill the bolt holes, then bolt the posts to the post anchors. Each one will consist of two parallel pieces of wood with one or more spacer blocks bolted between them to stabilise them.

13. The height of the posts will depend on the lie of the land; these ones range from 220 mm-1.55 m (8½ in-5 ft). You will need to sandwich only one spacer block between the uprights of the shorter posts, positioned at the base. In the case of the longer posts, insert a spacer block between the two uprights of each post at about 500 mm (1 ft 8 in) intervals to strengthen them.

STEP 14

14. Once all the posts have been positioned, mark on the posts the upper level of the substructure, where the slats will rest, using a water level (see page 10).

STEP 15

15. Check the posts frequently to ensure that they are plumb.

Completing the framework

16. If you cannot buy 6 m (19 ft 8 in) lengths of wood for the beams, use two 3 m (9 ft 10 in) lengths and connect them with a butt joint at the centre post. Position the first beam so that it lines up with the mark you have made (see step 14), with one end overhanging the end post, and the other end positioned midway through the centre post.

17. Clamp the post timbers firmly together. Use a spirit level or plumb bob to check that the wood is perfectly vertical, and then drill and bolt the timbers.

STEP 17

18. Using a circular saw (or a tenon saw if this is not available), cut any excess wood from the posts.

19. Sand the tops of the posts and beams with a belt sander.

STEP 18

STEP 19

STEP 20

20. Brace the beams and check, once again, that the posts are exactly vertical, as the substructure does often move slightly. Then attach the joists.

21. Position the ledgers between the posts and bolt them on to the base of the beams with hexagonal bolts, using a spanner to tighten the nuts. Make sure

STEP 21

STEP 22

STEP 27

that the timber is level or you will find that the joists provide an uneven support for the decking slats.

22. The joists should be set along the ledgers at approximately 500 mm (1 ft 8 in) centres.

23. Drill a skew hole on either side of each end of the joists and fasten the joists to the ledgers with the longer screws. This method will enable you to position the joists end to end on either side of the beams.

STEP 23

24. Fix a fascia board to either side of the structure, attaching it to each beam with three screws. If you are using shorter

lengths of wood, cut them to create a lap joint (as shown on page 27) and fasten them together with three 40 mm (1½ in) coach screws.

STEP 25

25. Where the joist rests on concrete, seal both surfaces with bitumen, and then secure the joists with angle brackets and 40 mm coach screws.

26. Using a 45° bit on a router, make a slight bevelled edge (5 mm; ¼ in) on each decking slat.

27. The procedure for attaching decking slats to the joists is exactly the same as described in steps 20-22 on page 40, except that screws are used here instead of stainless-steel nails. Since it is unlikely

that you will be able to get 6 m (19 ft 8 in) lengths of decking, alternate long and short pieces for effect. Use a 2.8 mm (⅛ in) drill bit to make pairs of holes along the slats at 545 mm (1 ft 9½ in) centres. Screw the decking slats in place, preferably using a screwdriver attachment on an electric drill.

Railings
28. Cut away a 220 mm x 25 mm (8½ in x 1 in) block from the base of each post. Position posts 1.2 m (3 ft 11 in) apart to the side of the deck.

STEP 29

29. Secure each post with two cuphead bolts, and use a spirit level to make sure that all posts are vertical.

30. The simplest railing consists of a series of posts attached to the side of the deck. If you prefer a criss-cross effect, position the timbers diagonally, joining each pair

STEP 30

STEP 31

STEP 33

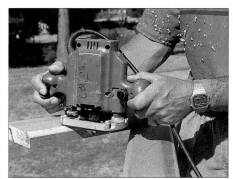

STEP 32

of crosspieces at the centre with a lap joint. To do this, cut out a block 48 mm x 11 mm (1⅞ in x ½ in) halfway down each crosspiece so that they slot together. To position the crosspieces, skew-screw them to the vertical timbers from underneath and above, using the shorter screws, and ensure that the bottom join is about 100 mm (4 in) from the deck surface.

Note that while 1.5 m (5 ft) lengths are specified, the exact lengths required may vary slightly, so it is best to cut the struts to size individually.

31. Before you attach the top railing and capping, fill all holes with epoxy or

a proprietary powder filler mixed with a little sawdust to colour it. The screw-holes in the decking slats can be filled at the same time.

32. Use a router to bevel the edges of the railing capping and create a more professional finish.

33. Screw the top rail (which holds the railing together) and the capping into place. Although short lengths abut each other, special joints are not necessary.

Finishing

34. Sand the filler and any rough edges, then seal or varnish the entire structure. When dry, sand lightly and seal again.

Timber furniture and an elegant canvas umbrella add the finishing touches to the pool deck.

PATIOS

Originally a patio was an inner courtyard, usually open to the sky, but this concept has evolved in such a way that modern patios are almost as varied as houses. Today the term 'patio' encompasses virtually any outdoor area for sitting or entertaining, from a paved area alongside the house to a terrace overlooking a swimming pool. Furthermore, these outdoor spaces may be either exposed to the weather or sheltered in some way. The one thing they all have in common, however, is a hard floor surface.

Once you have considered the primary uses for your patio and chosen a site for it, you will need to develop a suitable design and style for its construction. There are so many possibilities that this task can be daunting, but if you think of a patio as an outdoor room, conceptualising it will be a whole lot easier.

A useful rule of thumb, which should simplify matters further, is to follow an existing architectural or interior design theme. This applies not only to the floor surface, but to any related structures including pergolas, screen walls and built-in seating, as well as to colour schemes. If there is existing paving, it is usually best to match with it any bricks you use. This is especially important if the new surface is to adjoin an old one (see pages 57-58). Where this is not possible, choose a material that is complementary in colour and appearance; too much contrast can be visually confusing.

On the other hand, remember that rules can sometimes be broken. Even though a patio can be seen as an extension of the living rooms of a house, it may not lead directly from them. If you have a big garden and your new outdoor area is to be located at some distance from the house, you do not have to follow existing architectural features or match materials slavishly. Instead, you may be able to create an interestingly different area, using contrasting elements if you wish.

DESIGN

When designing a patio, aim for unity by planning the area in the context of your home and garden. A common mistake made by people designing their own gardens and patio areas is to try to create an exact copy of something they have seen elsewhere, which may not necessarily

suit the size and location of their property. Proportion is a particularly important aspect of good design – whatever you build should relate to the scale and size of your house and any existing features. In addition, soil and site conditions vary to such a degree that each situation must be considered on its own merits.

A landscape gardener will design a patio for you on paper, taking all other elements of the garden into account. You can do the same, using graph paper to ensure that it is to scale. Although it is not necessary to draw the entire property, any

large rocks, trees, established flower beds and existing hard surfaces in the vicinity should all be included in the plan. The position of the sun at various times of day and the direction of prevailing winds should also be noted.

If you are going to include a barbecue, seating or perhaps brick planters in the design, you can cut out templates (just as you would when planning an interior scheme), making sure that they are to the same scale as your basic drawing. Move these templates around on the plan until you are happy with the layout.

A trellis supports climbing plants which give shade to a charming patio.

A hot-water spa and L-shaped swimming pool designed to make the most of a courtyard patio.

STYLE

Having decided on the basic design and style of your patio, you will have to choose suitable materials. If the architecture of your house is in a distinctive style, it is best to reflect this as closely as possible. If not, just keep to the general feel of the building. A rustic patio will often harmonise best with a cottage-style home, while a fairly formal approach will be more appropriate if the house is modern in style.

Special features will often contribute to the mood that you are trying to create. For instance, a period-style gazebo and latticework can be used to evoke a Victorian ambience, while whitewashed walls and arches around a patio will help to create a Mediterranean look. Pots and planters suit most designs, although they go particularly well with a country look.

Before making your final choice, bear in mind that the surface materials you choose will also affect the style. Cobbles tend to give a rustic feel, while tiles will usually create a cleaner, more formal appearance. Brick paving will go with most styles, but choose the colour of it

Poles have been effectively used to give shelter to a Mediterranean-style barbecue patio.

A patio structure built to complement the Victorian-style architecture of the house. Canvas blinds may be rolled down for additional shelter.

Brick paving has been combined with concrete for the floor of this tranquil, leafy patio.

carefully. Used in a Mediterranean-style environment, for instance, red or terracotta is often a good choice.

THE PATIO FLOOR

The surface you choose for your patio floor will depend on a number of factors, including its primary function, the style and finish you want, and cost. While brick paving (see pages 12-13 and 23-25) is a popular choice and is safe for most patios, there are numerous other options ranging from cobblestones to timber and tiles.

Always ensure that the material you choose is suited to the location, and that you use the appropriate installation methods. Price must never be the only factor; consider visual effect and ease of laying (especially if you are going to do the work yourself). Laying any material which requires a concrete-slab base will inevitably mean an increase in the cost and effort involved in the project.

If the patio is to be used for entertaining or simply as a place to sit and relax, you will want a material which will provide you with a firm, level finish; if it is adjacent to a swimming pool, the material should also have a non-slip surface. You may be able

Old, weathered railway sleepers have been used alongside this swimming pool to create a rustic feel.

to go for a more unusual look with ground-cover plants, gravel or pebbles if it is simply a visually attractive area, at an entrance or in a courtyard, for instance.

Whatever material you decide to use on the floor should complement those used elsewhere on the property. Colours should tone in with each other, and textures should be compatible. Aim for a surface which is weather-resistant and easy to maintain. Although outdoor brickwork is not usually sealed, there are products available for sealing paving and unglazed tiles. A 50:50 mixture of linseed oil and turpentine may also be used on these surfaces to bring out the colour.

Bricks and blocks

Concrete and clay paving bricks come in a huge range of colours, from brick red, terracotta and the orange and brown autumn hues of natural clay, to grey, pink and charcoal. Both types can be laid on sand, concrete or mortar (see pages 24-25). As with any other kind of paving, you will need to work on a solid, well-compacted base regardless of the method you are using. Interlocking paving blocks are also suitable, particularly those which can be combined with planting (see pages 12-13).

Concrete sleepers edge a pool, while an adjacent patio is surfaced with simulated stone pavers.

Gravel can make a surprisingly attractive patio surface.

availability, expensive. Reconstituted stone flagstones are easier to come by, and are an ideal alternative to the real thing.

Alternatively, irregular pieces of cut stone or slate may be set on a concrete base in the form of crazy paving. Quantities required will depend on what is available; most suppliers will make a rough estimate of how much you will need to cover a given area.

Tiles

If your patio leads from a tiled interior, the obvious thing to do is to continue this surface, but first make sure that the tiles are suitable for outdoor use. If necessary, check that they are frost-resistant. For safety reasons, they should also have a matt, non-slip surface. Slate, natural clay tiles (including terracotta) and terrazzo, made from marble and stone chips set in concrete, are the most suitable. While marble and granite tiles are usually too highly polished to be practical outdoors, travertine, which looks a bit like marble, is another suitable option.

Although tiles are a reasonably popular choice for a patio which adjoins a house, they are not often used as a surface material elsewhere in the garden – a concrete slab has to be thrown before tiles of any kind can be laid.

While some tiles can be laid using a cement slush (a cement and water mixture), ceramic tiles should be laid on a screed using a cement-based adhesive (see pages 63-64). In both instances, grout is used in the joints.

Timber

In addition to decking, timber may also be used as a flooring material for patios. Old railway sleepers are an attractive and unusual choice. Made from extremely hard woods, they have already weathered for many years and will last for a long time to come. Although the surface of old sleepers is generally somewhat uneven, it is usually regular enough for seating and other furniture. The main disadvantages of railway sleepers are that the wood tends to become slippery in wet weather and that they are not always easily available.

Round sections of wood sliced from tree trunks are another attractive option which you can either cut yourself or purchase commercially. If you happen to be felling trees, this is a cheap choice, but be warned that they do eventually decay and will have to be replaced. As with timber sleepers, they can be slippery when wet, so grow a ground cover between them or place them in gravel to minimise the danger of slipping on them.

Concrete paving slabs

Although concrete may easily be cast *in situ*, companies manufacture a huge range of precast concrete products these days, many of which are designed specifically for the DIY market. Although the cheapest concrete products are plain grey and untextured, slabs and flagstones are often coloured for effect; others are finished with pebbles or a similar aggregate exposed decoratively on the surface. Slabs made from reconstituted or reconstructed stone are also available, usually in various sizes.

Concrete paving slabs can be laid either on a bed of sand or in mortar on a solid concrete base. They generally look best when combined with other materials, such as stone chips, small white pebbles or flowering ground covers.

In order to work out how many paving slabs you will need, first measure the site, then divide the area planned for the patio by the area of one slab (or the total area of different slabs or different materials), remembering to allow for the joints between the slabs.

Cobbles and setts

From a functional point of view, genuine cobblestones (rounded river stones) are not the best choice – they create a very irregular surface which is uncomfortable to walk on and ill-suited to moveable furniture, pot plants and so on. Genuine granite setts may be hard to come by and therefore expensive, so although they were often used for public pathways in the past, they are seldom seen in private gardens today.

However, an increasing number of companies now manufacture imitation cobbles and setts, which are flatter and more regular, from reconstituted stone and concrete. Although laying genuine cobbles is rather labour-intensive, as it involves pressing them individually into mortar on a solid concrete base, the techniques used for laying manufactured cobbles are the same as for slabs.

Slate and flagstone

Regular flagstones make an excellent surface for a patio, but they may be difficult to find and, depending on

A compact, brick-paved patio leads on to a green lawn.

A screeded concrete floor blends with natural rock.

Rustic brick paving and a reed ceiling add charm to this patio.

Ground cover grows through concrete strips cast in situ.

PATIO FOR ENTERTAINING

With built-in seating, this patio leading from a living room is the perfect place for entertaining. In this case the area chosen was already contained by walls on all sides, so there was no need to peg out the site or lay edging. This also made the location ideal for true flexible paving – bricks laid on a bed of sand with extra sand brushed between the joints. The step-by-step instructions given here will enable you not only to lay the paving but also to build the bench, side table and planter, all of which add character to the area.

STEP 4

Materials
To pave about 20 m² (24 sq yd):
900 paving bricks
0.8 m³ (1 cu yd) sand

For the built-in seat, table and planter:
50 bricks
12 paving bricks
50 kg (110 lb) cement
270 kg or 0.2 m³ (600 lb or ¼ cu yd) sand
135 kg (300 lb) stone
1 x 500 mm (1 ft 8 in) PVC pipe, 100 mm (4 in) in diameter
3 x 3 m x 150 mm x 38 mm (10 ft x 6 in x 1½ in) lengths of wood
4 x 450 mm x 150 mm x 38 mm (1 ft 6 in x 6 in x 1½ in) lengths of wood
12 x 60 mm (2½ in) brass screws

Preparation
1. Remove all rubble and vegetation from the area. Level the surface so that there is a drainage slope of about 1:40, falling away from the house. The ground level was raised to build this enclosed patio, and if you wish to do the same, compact the area between the walls and fill it with hardcore.

Foundations
2. Compact the entire surface thoroughly with a ramming tool (the one used here was made by welding a flat, heavy piece of metal to the end of a pole). It takes time to do this manually; for quicker results a compacting machine could be used.

STEP 2

3. Before paving begins, set out the foundations for the bench, table and planter. Use a builder's square to ensure that they are at right angles to the walls of the house and patio. Set up a builder's line with pegs or nails and string.

STEP 3

4. Dig three foundation trenches to a depth of 150 mm (6 in), as indicated on the diagram, and remove the soil.

5. Compact the soil in the trenches and dampen it so that not too much of the water from the concrete mix is absorbed into the ground.

6. Mix concrete in a 1:4:4 cement:sand: stone ratio. Using a shovel, pour enough concrete into the trenches to fill them to ground level. To ensure natural drainage, place two bricks in the centre of the planter foundation and remove them when the concrete sets, but before it hardens completely. Leave the foundations to set thoroughly for at least 24 hours – preferably longer.

STEP 6

Building the seating and planter

7. Mix mortar in a wheelbarrow or on a level surface, using a cement:sand ratio of 1:4. Add water little by little – too much will cause the cement to float, and if there is not enough, the mixture will be stiff, porous and unmanageable.

8. Following the basic bricklaying instructions described on pages 22-23, lay the first course of bricks using a builder's square and spirit level to make sure that the walls are absolutely plumb, level and square.

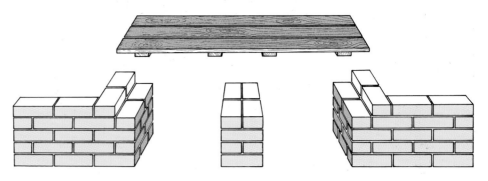

STEP 8

9. Build up the centre and inner walls (see diagram) to four courses and the walls around the perimeter of both table and planter to five courses. You can add one more course of bricks if you want the seat to be a little higher. Remember that once the paving has been laid, this will effectively lower the height of the bench.

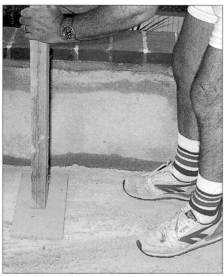

STEP 10

11. Position bricks over a surface area of about 2 m² (2¼-2½ sq yd) and tap firmly into place with a rubber mallet. Leave a slight gap between the bricks rather than abutting them directly. Use your spirit level frequently to ensure that you maintain the required drainage slope. Do this by setting the level on a straightedge; the bubble should be just off centre. For instructions on how to cut bricks, see page 25.

STEP 12

12. If, as in the case of this patio, the area is already surrounded by walls, knock a hole in the brickwork on the downward side of the drainage slope and insert the pipe. Fill the gaps with mortar to secure it.

13. Spread sand over the surface and sweep it in to fill all the joints. Hose the paving down lightly, then sprinkle a little more sand where necessary.

STEP 9

Paving

10. Spread a 25-30 mm (1 in) bed of sand over the entire area. Rake it out roughly and then compact and level it with a wooden punner. This is less back-breaking than using a straightedge, which is the other option (see page 10). Since you will have to walk on the sand, smooth only one section at a time.

STEP 11

STEP 13

STEP 14

STEP 16

STEP 17

Finishing the seating and planter

14. Smooth the wood with an orbital sander. You could use a router to round off the front edge if you wish. Give each piece a coat of sealant.

15. Lay the three planks side-by-side on a flat surface, leaving a 10 mm (½ in) gap between them.

16. Position the four shorter lengths of wood across the planks, as indicated on the diagram. Drill holes in them and screw them into place.

17. Varnish or seal the wood; leave to dry.

18. Slot the bench into place over the brickwork; the supporting timbers will stop it from slipping.

A useful built-in bench and brick side table on the completed patio encourage an outdoor lifestyle.

POOLSIDE PATIO

A sloping lawn which originally lay alongside a swimming pool was levelled and paved, using the hybrid method of paving, to make it more functional. Planters and a seating arrangement could easily be included by following the guidelines on pages 52-54.

Materials

To pave about 25 m² (30 sq yd):
1,125 paving bricks or blocks
1 m³ (1¼ cu yd) sand
150 kg (330 lb) cement
25 m² (30 sq yd) 150 micron
   plastic sheeting (optional)

Preparation

1. Peg out the area to be paved and remove all stones and vegetation, taking care to dig out any roots.

STEP 1

2. Excavate and level the site, allowing for about 25-30 mm (1 in) of sand for the bed plus a further 50-80 mm (2-3 in), depending on the thickness of the pavers. If the soil is unstable or you are building on a slope, you will also need to spread a layer of hardcore or take other special steps (see page 20), so remember to excavate to a greater depth.

3. Spread hardcore or gravel, if necessary, and then compact the entire area, allowing a very slight slope away from any buildings for drainage. If you wish, cover the ground or compacted hardcore with plastic sheeting (see page 24), overlapping the plastic at the edges and securing all ends with loose bricks.

STEP 3

Edging

4. Since the paving is to be laid on sand, the edging is vital to keep it in place, and the bricks around the perimeter should be set in mortar. Although not all the edgings should be laid at this stage, it is advisable to lay two sides, and start paving from these edges. First mix cement and sand in a 1:4 ratio, and use a trowel to lay a strip of mortar about 25 mm (1 in) high and 250 mm (10 in) wide.

STEP 4

5. Butter one edge of each brick with mortar and push it gently into the strip of mortar you have just laid. Tap the bricks with a rubber mallet or trowel handle; if any of the bricks are still too high, remove them and scrape a little of the mortar away. Use a spirit level to make sure that the horizontal surface is level, and a builder's square at all corners to check right angles and to ensure that the line you are forming is absolutely straight.

STEP 5

Laying the sand base

6. Now spread 25-30 mm (1 in) of sand over the plastic so that it is level with the top of the mortar which holds the edging in place.

STEP 6

7. Working in manageable sections, compact and smooth the sand by drawing a straight-edged piece of wood firmly across the surface. Keep checking with a spirit level to ensure that you have a slight slope for drainage. Although the exact gradient is not important, aim for a fall of about 1:40.

STEP 7

Paving

8. Decide on a pattern (see pages 23 and 24) and start working systematically from one end of the patio. Push each brick gently into the sand, and use a rubber mallet to tap it firmly into place. If any brick seems lower than the others, lift it up and pack a little extra sand beneath it. To cut bricks, see page 25.

STEP 8

9. Once all the paving bricks are in place, sweep a very weak, crumbly mixture of cement and sand (mixed in a 1:6 ratio) over the surface in order to fill any gaps.

STEP 9

Finishing off

10. Using a hose, spray the newly paved area lightly with water, then brush the surface and flush with clean water to remove all traces of mortar and prevent ugly staining. It is best to allow the cement to dry thoroughly, for a few days, before using the patio.

The completed paving provides a hard, practical patio surface adjacent to the swimming pool.

PATIO EXTENSION

Although the existing paved area leading from this house was adequate, extending the paving seemed a good option when a pergola was built to create some shade (see pages 84-86). The original dimensions of the patio were 3.5 m x 5.4 m (11 ft 6 in x 17 ft 8 in), and by adding a strip 2 m (6 ft 6 in) wide down one side and incorporating a pathway, the area was increased from about 19 m² (23 sq yd) to 34 m² (40 sq yd). Since rigid paving had been used in the original patio, the concrete slab had to be extended before the bricks could be laid on a bed of mortar.

Materials
To extend paving by 15 m² (18 sq yd):
675 paving bricks to match
  existing surface
400 kg (880 lb) cement
1 m³ (1¼ cu yd) sand
1 m³ (1¼ cu yd) stone

STEP 1

Preparation
1. Mark out the area to be paved using lime, white cement, chalk or even flour. The concrete slab should extend about 150 mm (6 in) beyond the planned edge of the paving.

2. Now dig out all the grass and remove the sods. Excavate the ground to the same depth as the bottom of the existing concrete slab.

3. Level the area to continue the drainage slope of the adjacent surface.

4. Remove the edging of the old patio where the new paving will join it. All half-bricks will also have to be dislodged. Use a club hammer and a chisel to do this, firmly tapping each mortar joint to work the bricks loose. This takes a bit of time, but if you are careful, you will be able to reuse most of the bricks.

STEP 4

5. Rake away stones and other debris and compact the area well before mixing cement, sand and stone in the ratio 1:4:4 for the new concrete slab. Throw the slab as shown on pages 21-22, making sure that it matches the level of the existing slab. Make sure that you allow for about a 10 mm (½ in) layer of mortar on which to lay the pavers. Allow the concrete slab to set properly.

Jointing rigid paving
6. There are several ways in which you can joint rigid paving (see pages 24-25), but in the method used here, the bricks are bedded and jointed at the same time. Working in bands of about half a metre (1 ft 8 in), place mortar mixed in a 1:4 cement:sand ratio on the concrete with a trowel.

7. Then butter each brick just as you would for bricklaying and push the paver into the mortar bed, using the dimensions of the existing joints as a guide. Additional mortar may be pushed into the joints with a trowel. If necessary, tap the pavers with the trowel handle to level them. This process is time-consuming, but it is worth the effort if you want to achieve a really professional finish. Use a spirit level frequently to check the drainage slope and ensure that the paving is even.

8. When you get to the end of the patio, you will have to cut bricks to create a straight line (see page 25).

Edging the paving

9. Although it is not as important to have edge restraints for rigid paving as for bricks laid on sand, a solid edging will finish off the paving neatly and prevent bricks from breaking away from the mortar bed. Place a row of whole bricks along the edge, buttering each brick as described in step 7.

Finishing off

10. Once you have finished paving the whole area, check that all the joints are properly filled. If there are still spaces, use a trowel to place a little more mortar in between the bricks, taking care not to smear mortar on the paving.

STEP 7

STEP 9

A patio extension which gives the owners an additional 15 m² (18 sq yd) of practical, outdoor living space.

FLAGSTONE PATIO

Simulated stone slabs may be used to create an attractive patio in a corner of the garden. For this simple project, three different sizes of paver are used to create a random design, giving the area a charming, rustic feel, while pebbles scattered between the artificial flagstones add an interesting finishing touch. A similar effect could be created with ordinary concrete slabs or real stone. In this case, the patio is contained by timber on one side, but if you do not plan to have such an edging, excavate to a level which will ensure that the finished surface is flush with the ground.

Laying the sand base

3. Spread 25-50 mm (1-2 in) sand over the patio area and hose down lightly. The water will help to compact the surface, making it easier for you to level it.

4. Using a spirit level (on its own or placed on a straightedge), smooth out the sand. If the patio is next to a building, the floor surface should slope slightly away from it, and should be at least 150 mm (6 in) below the DPC under the floor slab.

Laying the slabs

5. Start laying the slabs from the furthest corner, leaving a slight gap between each. There is no particular pattern to be followed – simply place them as you feel they look most attractive, ensuring that you have a good mix of sizes throughout. Tap gently with a rubber mallet to level them. To avoid disturbing the sand you have already smoothed out and levelled, it is a good idea to use a couple of slabs as temporary stepping stones.

Materials

For a 3.6 m x 3.2 m (12 ft x 10 ft 6 in) patio:
23 x 500 mm x 500 mm (1 ft 8 in x 1 ft 8 in) slabs
23 x 500 mm x 250 mm (1 ft 8 in x 10 in) slabs
23 x 250 mm x 250 mm (10 in x 10 in) slabs
0.6 m³ (¾ cu yd) sand
40 kg (88 lbs) of 13 mm (½ in) pebbles

Preparation

1. If the patio is not enclosed, peg out the area. Level the ground.

2. If the soil is stable, compact it now; otherwise spread a layer of hardcore to form a solid sub-base before compacting.

STEP 4

STEP 3

STEP 5

STEP 7

6. Once all the slabs are in place, check that you are happy with the configuration you have achieved. If there are large gaps in some places, adjust the stones now for a better fit.

7. Spread sand over the surface and brush it loosely in between the pavers. Then hose the area down lightly to compact it.

Finishing off
8. Spread pebbles over the surface and brush into place. Once the pebbles have settled, add more if and where necessary. If you want to give the patio a more informal look, sow some flower seed between the slabs.

STEP 8

A previously unused corner of the garden is transformed by the addition of a flagstone patio.

COBBLED PATIO

Regular man-made cobbles or setts create a delightfully rustic effect in a small courtyard. The skills required for laying cobblestones are basically the same as for other types of paving, but this is a particularly simple project as their small size makes them easy to handle. Although the setts were laid in a straightforward grid in this project, they could also be staggered to create a stretcher bond pattern.

STEP 4

Materials
To lay about 10 m² (12 sq yd) of cobbles or setts:
800 x 110 mm x 110 mm x 50 mm (4¼ in x 4¼ in x 2 in) cobbles or setts
0.5 m³ (¾ cu yd) sand
50 kg (110 lb) cement

Preparation
1. Clear the area, making sure that you remove all weeds, grass, stones and excess soil. Since this is a courtyard adjacent to the house, there is no need to set out the site, but it is important to excavate to a depth of at least 200 mm (8 in) below the level of DPC. This will ensure that the top of the setts, which are 50 mm (2 in) deep, is far enough below the floor level. If hardcore is required, you will obviously have to remove more soil to accommodate it.

2. Compact the surface thoroughly, ensuring that the ground slopes away from the building.

Bare grass and a small section of badly laid paving do little to enhance a small courtyard.

STEP 3

Laying the sand base
3. Cover the area with about 40 mm (1½ in) of sand. Rake and smooth it as described on page 59.

Laying the cobbles or setts
4. If you are laying the cobbles or setts in an enclosed area, start laying them alongside one wall. Tap each cobble or sett gently into the sand bed with a rubber mallet. However, if the patio is not bounded by any walls, first spread a strip of mortar along one side (as described in step 6) to hold the edges in place.

5. Continue laying the cobbles or setts in a straight grid or stretcher bond pattern, as desired. Check the levels frequently to ensure that they are laid as evenly as possible. If any are lower than the others, lift them and put a little extra sand under them. Even though they are factory-made, artificial cobbles or setts may not be exactly the same size, so the gaps between them will not always be consistent.

6. Wherever the outside edge is not bounded by a wall, you will need to hold it in place with mortar. Use a 1:4

STEP 5

STEP 6

STEP 7

cement:sand mix and spread the concrete with a bricklayer's trowel. Press the cobbles or setts firmly into position.

Finishing off
7. Now make a dry mixture of cement and sand in the same ratio and brush it into the joints.

8. Sprinkle a little water on to the surface and continue brushing in the cement:sand mix until all the joints are flush with the top of the paving.

9. Try not to leave any traces of mortar on the surface – once it dries it can be very difficult to remove. If you do spot

any excess, wipe it off with a cloth or sponge. This may seem tedious, but if you try to hose down the cobbles or setts before the mortar has set, you will simply wash it out of the joints. If the cobbles or setts are not made of concrete, remove any excess mortar following the instructions given on page 25.

Cobbles or setts transform the courtyard and create a charming atmosphere.

TILED PATIO

Tiles are a particularly good choice for finishing a suspended concrete deck or a patio raised above ground level. In this instance, tiling was used in order to continue the surface used within the house. Since the interior tiles had a glazed matt surface and were suitable for outdoor use, exactly the same ones were chosen for the patio. If you are planning to tile an open-sided patio at ground level, it is a good idea to make sure that the dimensions of the floor surface accommodate whole tiles in order to avoid cutting.

STEP 6

7. Now mark a second line, using the 3:4:5 method (as shown on page 19) to ensure that it crosses the first at exactly 90°. This is essential for a professional finish.

Materials
To screed and tile 16.25 m²
(19½ sq yd):
162 x 320 mm x 320 mm (180 x 12 in x 12 in) tiles
135 kg (300 lb) cement
0.5 m³ (½ cu yd) sand
bonding agent (optional)
40 kg (88 lb) cement-based tile adhesive
10 kg (22 lb) grout

Preparation
1. If you have a suspended concrete deck and there are rooms or a garage below, you may well have to seal the surface of the deck before you screed and tile it. It is in any case a wise precaution to take, as waterproofing at a later stage is a tedious and often costly task. There are various products you can use, although bitumen is a popular and proven one.

2. Once bitumen has dried completely, it is essential to apply a suitable bonding solution before screeding.

Laying the screed
3. Mix the mortar for the screed using a cement:sand ratio of 1:4 and pour it on to the surface.

4. Use a straightedge to scrape the mortar across the floor, checking frequently with a spirit level to ensure that it slopes slightly away from any adjoining house walls (see pages 19 and 20).

STEP 5

5. Use a wooden float to get a uniform surface, and a steel float to get a smooth finish. Allow the screed to set thoroughly, preferably for two or three days. To aid curing, keep the surface damp by spraying the surface with water.

Preparing the surface
6. If the patio is bounded by walls and leads off the house, start laying the tiles from the outside edge. This will keep cutting to a minimum and all cut tiles will be alongside the house. Alternatively, work from the centre of the patio. Either way, mark the position of the first row of tiles with a chalk line. If there is an existing edging, or if you are tiling alongside a wall, check that the corners are square. If they are, you can use this edging or wall as a guide.

Laying the tiles
8. Brush all loose cement off the surface before you start tiling. Mix the tile

STEP 7

STEP 8

STEP 9

adhesive with water according to the manufacturer's instructions. Spread a 6 mm (¼ in) layer over an area of not more than 1 m² (1 sq yd) at a time, using a notched trowel which will form ridges for maximum adhesion.

9. Position the straightedge along the chalk line as a guide and press each tile firmly into position. Knock the tiles gently with a rubber mallet to level them. Remove any excess adhesive from the surface of the tiles before it dries.

STEP 10

10. Use spacers (see page 10) to ensure an even gap for grouting. Also use your square from time to time to check that you are maintaining 90° angles.

Cutting tiles

11. To determine where a tile should be cut, line each one up with the edge of the patio and the last section of tiles you have laid. Mark with a pencil before cutting.

STEP 11

STEP 12

12. The simplest way to cut tiles for awkward corners or edges is to use a tile-cutting machine. Score the surface of the tile, then press the handle down firmly to break it in two. If you do not have a tile-cutting machine, you could hire one, as scoring and breaking the tiles by hand will probably result in a lot of unnecessary breakage. If you are laying quarry tiles, it is worth using an angle grinder instead.

Grouting

13. Allow the tile adhesive to dry thoroughly, at least overnight, before grouting. Mix the grout according to the manufacturer's instructions and spread over the surface, carefully working it into the joints.

Finishing off

14. Using a large sponge, wipe away any excess grout before it dries.

STEP 13

The tiled floor surface gives this patio a sleek, sophisticated appeal.

STEPS AND PATHS

Steps and paths are found in just about every garden, no matter how small. While steps allow access between different levels, paths link the house with outbuildings and various parts of the garden. Both are thus important parts of deck and patio design. Well planned and imaginatively constructed, they can be practical and attractive additions to any outdoor area.

Because timber decks are always at least partly raised, steps are essential if one wants access to the ground below. Many decks are split-level, so steps can be an integral part of their design. Patios, too, are sometimes slightly elevated, so one or two steps may need to be built for comfortable access to and from the garden. In sloping gardens, steps can be built to lead people from one terrace to another.

Where a patio or deck is located away from the house, a pathway is usually necessary to provide safe and convenient access between the house and any outdoor living areas, as well as to prevent grass from becoming trodden away in places. If the deck or patio is adjacent to the house, a path will often lead from it into the garden.

STEPS

Many gardens have their ups and downs, and the most common way of dealing with them is to build steps. These are not merely functional structures, and they should be considered as a part of the garden design as a whole.

Although safety and ease of use are always primary factors to bear in mind when designing stairs, the visual effect of a stairway must also be taken into account, and proportions are vital. A steep, narrow staircase may be your only option in a confined area, but it may also not entice one to explore further. If they are more generously proportioned, on the other hand, stairs can be much more inviting and easier to use.

Dimensions

Accepted dimensions for an interior staircase combine treads of at least 250 mm (10 in) with risers up to 200 mm (8 in) high. Treads for garden stairs, though, are often as deep as 450 mm (1 ft 6 in), with risers as short as 130 mm (5 in). If treads are any deeper than this,

Timber steps lead from a wooden jetty to a multilevel deck above.

Brick steps leading from a house match the paved patio surface.

however, there should, if at all possible, be sufficient space for a person to take two steps on each tread – or you could consider laying a path instead.

Materials

It is often possible to use the same materials for both steps and pathways. Brick and concrete (including both precast slabs and concrete cast *in situ*) are particularly common choices, as they are relatively cheap and easy to install and maintain. These materials may also be combined – for example, brick risers with concrete slab treads, or concrete blocks (see pages 70-71) with plastered risers and tiled treads.

A more rustic look can be achieved by using natural materials such as railway sleepers or cut stone.

PATHS

A garden path can be more than just a link between parts of your property: like steps, a path can also become an attractive feature in your outdoor design.

If, for instance, the path leads to a secluded patio some distance from the house, you can create an inviting, winding walkway which disappears from view behind established shrubs and trees. If you have a formal, symmetrical garden plan and patio or deck, it would probably be more appropriate to opt for a pathway planned along similar lines.

Materials

In terms of appearance, often the best choice is to match the materials for the path with those used in the areas it links. Brick paving, flagstones, concrete slabs and imitation setts are all good surfaces for pathways. Although tiles are less common, there is no reason why they should not be used, provided that they have a non-slip surface. You will also have to cast a concrete base before you can lay them.

Instead of a continuous pathway, you may prefer stepping stones. Various precast products are suitable, including square or round concrete slabs, some of which have an exposed aggregate surface, imitation flagstone or pieces of cut stone, and simulated logs or sleepers. Timber is another option: as with other kinds of stepping stone, railway sleepers and rounds cut from tree trunks can both be laid with ground-cover plants or grass planted between them, as well as on their own to form a continuous surface. When laying any material with grass or a ground cover in between the units, bear in mind that you will probably have to trim the planting fairly frequently.

A profile, made from two straight-edged pieces of wood joined at right angles, will enable you to work out how many steps you need. The vertical length indicates the change in level and the horizontal measurement, the depth of the slope. Alter one or other of the lengths if you do not have a suitable tread/riser combination.

A wide stepping-stone walkway leads to some brick steps.

Railway sleepers are an attractive option for steps with a rustic feel.

FACEBRICK PATIO STEPS

Since this patio features a facebrick planter, seat and table to match the flooring, the steps were built of the same brick. Alternatively, one could pave the treads and plaster the risers. Exact quantities of materials will depend on the levels in your garden and the number of steps required. This project details the procedure to be followed for building three steps about 1.5 m (5 ft) wide with 200 mm (8 in) high risers and 450 mm (1 ft 6 in) treads.

Materials
80 plaster bricks
80 facebricks
80 paving bricks
120 kg (265 lb) cement
540 kg or 0.4 m³ (1,190 lb or ½ cu yd) sand
75 kg (165 lb) stone
0.8 m³ (1 cu yd) fill

Preparation
1. Peg out the area the steps will fill – in this case, 1.6 m x 1.35 m (5 ft 3 in x 4 ft 5 in). When working on a slope, a simple profile (see illustration on page 67) makes this task easier.

2. Knock nails or pegs into the ground to mark the planned surface of the step foundation; the foundation will be 50 mm (2 in) deep, and its top surface flush with the ground. Check them with a spirit level.

3. If you are stepping a slope, you will have to remove some of the soil. Rather than cutting away the whole area, work out the level of each step and excavate the general shape. Remove all vegetation and level the area, then compact it to create a good, firm base.

Foundation
4. If you are building steps leading from one flat surface to another, it is best to throw a single foundation slab before construction commences. Mix concrete using a cement:sand:stone ratio of 1:4:4, and throw the foundation slab. To do this, you will need about half a bag of cement.

5. Compact the wet concrete with a straightedge, using a chopping action. Stop when pasty cement begins to come to the surface. To level the surface, draw the plank towards you with a side-to-side sawing motion. Allow the concrete to set thoroughly for at least 48 hours, keeping it moist.

6. Although most professional bricklayers appear to work on instinct, it is always safer to mark out the area of the steps with chalk or pencil on the dry concrete. Use a builder's square to make sure that the lines are perpendicular, as this will help you to lay supporting walls for the steps accurately.

STEP 7

Side walls
7. Mix cement and sand in the ratio 1:4 for the mortar. Start laying stepped one-brick side walls (see page 12), using plaster bricks on the inside (to cut down costs) and facebricks on the outside. Spread a strip of mortar on the surface of the foundation and lay the first row of bricks. When laying the following and subsequent courses, cover the top surface of the wall with mortar and furrow it with the trowel. Butter one end of each brick and slide them into position on the mortar. Tap into place with the trowel handle, and scrape off any excess mortar.

STEP 8

Risers
8. Draw a line parallel to the back wall, 450 mm (1 ft 6 in) from the wall, to mark the front edge of the first (top) tread. Using plaster bricks, lay four courses of

STEP 3

STEP 5

a half-brick wall along the whole length of the step, with the front edge of the brickwork lying along the line you have just marked. Lay one more course with facebricks to form the top riser (or two if the top riser is to be the same height as the others).

9. Repeat the previous step, building two courses with plaster bricks and two with facebricks. The third wall, which forms the front riser, should be only two courses high and built of facebrick only, as all the brickwork will be visible when the steps are finished. A builder's line will help to ensure that each course is straight.

STEP 9

10. Complete both side walls, so that they match the heights of the three risers. Use a spirit level to check that the horizontal and vertical surfaces of the brickwork are all straight and level.

Treads

11. Allow the mortar to dry before shovelling broken bricks, stones, soil and any other fill into the gaps between the walls which form the risers.

STEP 11

12. Compact the fill well. Top it with a thin layer of weak (1:6) cement:sand mixture, and water it lightly to ensure that it fills any gaps in the rubble or soil.

STEP 13

13. Lay paving bricks on the surface of each tread. Butter the bricks with mortar as you work, and use a trowel to fill any remaining joints.

STEP 14

Finishing

14. Since this is a small area, sprinkle dry building sand over the steps, then rub gently but firmly with a dry piece of sponge to remove any wet mortar from the newly paved surface. If there are any stains, treat them as described on page 25 once the mortar has dried.

The facebrick steps provide safe access between the patio and the interior of the house.

CONCRETE BLOCK STEPS

When steps are to be plastered, inexpensive concrete blocks make an ideal building material. Although the basic method is the same as for building brick steps, the final result is quite different. This project, which also includes the construction of simple planters, illustrates how blocks can be used to link two patio areas which are on different levels. Blocks are manufactured in a variety of sizes and you may have to alter the materials list accordingly. Here, hollow concrete blocks were used to build four steps 1.5 m (5 ft) wide. Treads are 400 mm (1ft 4 in) deep and risers are 200 mm (8 in) high, that is, the length and height of a block plus mortar joint.

STEP 6

Materials
45 x 390 mm x 190 mm x 190 mm
  (15 in x 7½ in x 7½ in) hollow
  concrete blocks
106 kg (233 lb) cement
14 kg (31 lb) lime (optional)
475 kg or 0.35 m³ (1,040 lb or
  ½ cu yd) sand
220 kg (485 lb) stone
0.9 m³ (1¼ cu yd) fill
500 g (8 oz) oxide pigment

Preparation
1. Measure the area allocated for the steps and, if possible, choose blocks which will fit the space without requiring cutting.

2. Lay out the blocks without mortar. This will help you to determine the level of each step and work out the number of blocks needed. When building steps up to a raised area, the top course of blocks should be level with that area or one step down. Excavate a little if necessary.

3. Make a gauge rod indicating the height of the block plus mortar joint (190 mm + 10 mm; 7½ in + ½ in) for a few courses, and hold it up against the wall. This will show you how high the top of the foundation should be.

4. Clear the site, removing any stones and vegetation.

5. Excavate to a depth of 50 mm (2 in), plus whatever additional depth you require to ensure that the top level of blocks will be flush with the patio – in this instance, about another 50 mm (2 in).

Foundations
6. Mix cement, sand and stone in the ratio 1:4:4, using just over half a bag of cement. Throw the foundation as described on pages 21–22, using a straightedge to compact the concrete.

Brickwork
7. Mix mortar, combining cement and sand in the ratio 1:6. With a trowel, place a small amount on top of the concrete

foundation. Lay the blocks, pushing them firmly into the mortar. Level them by adding or removing mortar as necessary; use the first line marked on your gauge rod as a guide. If the ground slopes, you may have to use bricks underneath the blocks in some places to get the first course absolutely level.

8. Having established where the steps will end, build the side and riser walls, using corner blocks and a line to ensure that they are straight.

STEP 8

9. Use a spirit level frequently to make sure that the walls are perfectly straight, horizontal and vertical, and that the top course and the paving are aligned.

Planters
10. If you are going to incorporate planters, first construct walls behind the risers, parallel to and a little way in from one side wall, to contain the fill behind the riser walls.

STEP 2

STEP 9

12. Mix and pour concrete on to the hardcore and sand in exactly the same way as you did for the step foundations. Alternatively, you could omit the hardcore and fill the space behind the walls with concrete from the ground up, but this would be a more costly exercise and one which is not really necessary.

Plaster or render

13. You will need just over half a bag of cement for the plaster or render. If the plaster sand does not contain lime, it is usually best to add builder's hydrated lime to the mix. The plaster or render, which should be 10-15 mm (⅜-½ in) thick, will also be less likely to crack. Apply it with a plasterer's trowel and then use a wooden float to get a smooth surface. A corner trowel will help neaten the edges.

14. When the plaster or render has set, mix the pigment powder with about a kilogram (2 lb) of cement and enough water to make a paste. Brush it on, using firm, even strokes, and taking care not to stain adjacent surfaces. A little of the colour will wash out over time, causing some mottling of the surface. For alternative methods, see page 22.

STEP 11

Finishing the steps

11. When the riser and planter walls are complete, fill in the space behind them with hardcore. Use sand or soil to fill any gaps in the hardcore, and then compact it well, leaving space for a 50 mm (2 in) layer of concrete.

STEP 13

Concrete steps, coloured with red iron oxide powder, connect the two levels of a brick patio.

MODULAR PRECAST CONCRETE STEPS AND RETAINING WALL

Interlocking concrete terrace blocks are manufactured in various shapes and sizes especially for retaining walls, and some can easily be used to make steps too. They are simply laid on their sides to form the treads, and filled with a very weak mortar mix for stability. This project combined both possibilities in the garden where the pool deck was constructed (see project on pages 41-45). Although the slope was not particularly steep, the earth was unstable, and building a retaining wall was the easiest way to stabilise it. In addition, blocks were laid along the 6 m (20 ft) long stairway, creating attractive planters. This is one of the simplest projects, and requires no special skills.

Preparation

1. Although it is not necessary to throw a concrete foundation, it is essential to prepare a level, well-compacted base for the retaining wall. Establish where the wall will start and excavate a trench about 600 mm (2 ft) wide and 6 m (20 ft) long.

2. Pile the soil on one side. Unless you have clay soil which does not drain well, this can be used to backfill the wall (see step 5). If you cannot use the existing soil, you will have to bring in an additional 1.2 m³ (1½ cu yd) of soil or sand.

3. Use a spirit level to check that the ground is flat before you start laying the blocks.

4. If the ground slopes, step the trench and use an extra course of blocks on the lower level.

Retaining wall

5. Start laying the blocks, leaving a gap of about 200 mm (8 in) between the excavated slope and the row of blocks. Lay them at a slight angle, so that each corner slots into the next. They must interlock to give the wall strength and stability, but since modular block designs vary, be sure to follow any manufacturer's instructions. The wall is backfilled with sand or soil, which is then compacted. If there is a

Materials

To build a retaining wall, 6 m (20 ft) long and 1 m (3 ft 3 in) high:
84 x 400 mm x 200 mm x 200 mm (1 ft 4 in x 8 in x 8 in) terrace blocks
0.7 m³ (1 cu yd) soil

To build the steps, 6 m (20 ft) long and 800 mm (2 ft 8 in) wide, and the planters:
116 x 400 mm x 200 mm x 200 mm (1 ft 4 in x 8 in x 8 in) terrace blocks
75 kg (165 lb) cement
405 kg (895 lb) sand

STEP 1

STEP 5

STEP 6

STEP 9

STEP 11

problem with water seepage or clay soil, you will need to incorporate a drainage layer of stone and river sand below the soil.

6. Once you have laid a course of blocks, fill them and the space behind them with fertile soil.

7. Lay the second row of blocks over the first, but slightly further back, so that the holes in the bottom blocks are partly visible. Once the wall is complete, these 'pockets' can be planted.

Steps
11. The steps can be as wide as you wish; four blocks in a row will result in a flight 800 mm (2 ft 8 in) wide. With an overlap of 20 mm (1 in), a single block tread of

380 mm (1 ft 3 in) is quite adequate, although a double row will work well on a gentle slope and where the steps curve. After positioning the blocks, shovel mortar into the hollow in each block.

STEP 8

8. Use a spirit level frequently to ensure that the horizontal surface is flat and level. A builder's line will help you keep the wall straight as you work.

9. Continue laying the blocks until the required height is reached.

10. A good way to ensure proper compaction is to water the soil-filled blocks once they are in position. Any gaps can be filled in with more soil.

STEP 10

12. Compact the soil behind each step and ensure that the ground is absolutely level before you start laying the next row of blocks. A home-made punner (see pages 10-11) is quite adequate for this purpose.

STEP 12

Planters

13. Lay additional blocks lengthways alongside the steps, with the hollows facing upward. Where necessary, stack them so that the blocks are higher than the treads.

14. Fill these blocks with fertile soil in order to create the planters.

STEP 14

15. If the steps curve, there will be gaps in some parts of the treads. Fill these gaps with mortar or plant a ground cover between the units.

Finishing

16. Plant the wall and the edging of the staircase with hardy creepers or climbers – and soon the structure will be covered in greenery.

Pockets of soil in the retaining wall have been planted to soften the appearance of the structure.

Terrace blocks along the edges of the steps have been laid to create planters.

TIMBER STEPS

Any type of deck built off the ground will require steps if you are going to have direct access to the garden or to another level. Although there are numerous ways to build steps, this project illustrates how to construct the simplest type of timber staircase: steps with an open riser. The same principle may be used for a staircase with a longer span, leading to a higher deck, although handrails would then be required for safety reasons. Should you wish to box in the tread, you will need to use longer cleats along the two stringers to support the riser boards.

Materials
2 x 1.3 m x 220 mm x 36 mm
(4 ft 3 in x 8½ in x 1½ in) pieces
of wood for the stringers
3 x 1.2 m x 220 mm x 36 mm
(4 ft x 8½ in x 1½ in) pieces of wood
for the treads
6 x 200 mm x 36 mm x 36 mm
(8 in x 1½ in x 1½ in) pieces of wood
for the cleats
30 x 60 mm (2¼ in) brass countersunk
screws
4 x 8 mm x 110 mm (⅜ in x 4¼ in)
coach screws
55 kg (120 lb) cement
225 kg (500 lb) sand
225 kg (500 lb) stone

Preparation
1. Check that the dimensions of the materials specified for this 850 mm (2 ft 9 in) high deck are appropriate for your site. If you are building steps to a deck, the height of the deck will be a major factor in determining the number of steps and, to some extent, the height of the risers.

2. To make the task easier, create a simple profile by nailing two battens together at right angles. The upright length of wood should match the height of the deck (in other words, the change in level), and the horizontal length should equal the depth of the slope. From this you should be able to work out the optimum number of steps for the site (see illustration on page 67).

3. Even though these steps are made from timber, it is best to concrete the bottom ends firmly into the ground to anchor them and prevent them from becoming unsteady. Having determined where the first step will be, dig two square holes approximately 200 mm x 300 mm (8 in x 12 in) across and 200 mm (8 in) deep.

Construction
4. First cut the stringers to size. These are the lengths of wood on either side of the steps that hold the treads in place. Cut the top of each stringer at the required angle, so that you can abut the stringers to the deck fascia. If the steps lead to a verandah or raised patio, you will have to secure the stringers to a ledger (see page 34), which must first be bolted on to the patio or verandah wall.

5. Paint the end of each stringer with bitumen to seal them underground.

6. Now mark the position of the cleats to which the treads will be nailed. In this instance, they are 260 mm (10 in) apart.

STEP 7

7. Use a combination square to ensure that each cleat is straight and level, and secure with the countersunk screws.

STEP 5

8. Position the stringer with one end in the hole you have dug, ensuring that the sides are plumb. Attach the top of each stringer to the deck with coach screws. Unless you attach it to the fascia before completing the deck, you will have to work from behind the fascia. Alternatively, use angle brackets.

9. Mix concrete using a cement:sand:stone ratio of 1:4:4 and pour it into the hole. Brace the stringers to hold them in position while the concrete dries.

10. Each tread consists of a 1.2 m (4 ft) length of wood. Position and screw the planks to the cleat.

Finishing
11. Fill all nail holes, as described on pages 26 and 45, then seal or varnish the timber.

STEP 9

STEP 10

The finished steps lead to a low-level DIY deck constructed alongside the house.

STEPPING-STONE PATH

Rather than having a solid pathway across a lawn, you could lay precast concrete stepping stones. However, you will have to be sure to keep the grass around them well clipped, or they will quickly become untidy and the effect will be lost. Since laying a stepping-stone path is simple and reasonably quick, it makes a perfect weekend project. In this case, the pathway provides access from the house to a barbecue patio.

STEP 3

Laying the stepping stones
4. Lay a 25 mm (1 in) bed of sand in each hole and compact it.

Materials
For a 6 m (20 ft) path:
11 stepping stones, 320 mm (12 in) in diameter
25 kg (55 lb) sand

Preparation
1. Lay the stepping stones out on top of the grass, about 200 mm (8 in) apart, and mark around them with chalk or flour.

STEP 2

3. The surface under the stepping stones must be flat and level. Although it is awkward working in holes, compact it as best you can. A home-made punner or a pole will do the job well.

STEP 4

5. Put the stepping stones in place. The finished surface of each stepping stone should be flush with the lawn. If they are below the surrounding ground, the grass will probably grow over them quickly. If they protrude above the lawn, people may trip over them. There is no need to cement the stepping stones in place as the earth around them will keep them in position.

STEP 1

2. Following the line you have marked, dig out grass and soil to a depth of about 75 mm (3 in). This will accommodate a 25 mm (1 in) bed of sand as well as the thickness of the stepping stone.

STEP 5

The completed stepping-stone path leads across the lawn to a barbecue patio.

OVERHEADS AND SCREENS

A well-planned deck or patio can effectively become an outdoor living room, and designing it so that there is some shade and shelter will help to make it really successful. Ideally the area should also be reasonably private – at least shielded from view of neighbours and passers-by. To achieve this, consider the possibility of incorporating some sort of overhead structure or screen in the overall design.

Adding an overhead structure, such as a pergola or awning, to a patio or deck can extend the area's usefulness dramatically. Frequently overheads simply provide shade, but a roof could also shelter the deck or patio from the rain.

Your needs will be determined partly by conditions in your garden. If the patio area is very windy, a screen wall or even an uncomplicated lattice screen could make all the difference, shielding you from prevailing winds. Properly planned, it will also provide some privacy.

Pergolas and other overhead structures will provide varying amounts of shelter, depending on the roof covering used. A solid roof will give good protection from all weather, while timber laths and awning materials will only create shade. A gazebo, if it suits the style of your house, could shelter a small patio (or part of a larger one) from both rain and sun.

Whatever type of shelter or screening is chosen, it is important to ensure that the materials and style suit your house and garden as well as the patio or deck itself. A screen erected alongside a deck should be made of the same type of timber as the deck, while a patio wall should ideally match existing brickwork.

DESIGN AND STYLE

You will probably decide on the design and style of the area as a whole before turning your attention to pergolas and screens, which are often considered to be of secondary importance. Bear in mind, though, that these structures can play a vital role in creating the visual character of the patio or deck. Of course, not all gardens and garden structures follow a particular style, but materials and proportion should always be central factors.

A brick-paved patio with no special features could be transformed by the addition of a Mediterranean-style pergola, with plastered and whitewashed columns

and a pole roof. A more solid roof can create a cosy, cottagey atmosphere, while latticework enhances a Victorian theme, and thick bamboo poles tend to give a Japanese look. Screens and walls can have a similar effect, so once again materials should be chosen with care.

Shrubs and hedges may be included in the scheme, and creepers planted over structures to soften the appearance of the patio and add contrast and interest.

You will be more limited when it comes to providing shade or screening on a deck, as sawn wood and split poles are virtually your only options. However, the design possibilities are endless, and by simply adding a screen or overhead you will give the structure a new dimension – as well as making it more practical.

A solid timber screen shields this narrow deck from the wind and creates privacy.

A rudimentary pole pergola topped with debarked sticks.

MATERIALS

Although the overhead structure of a pergola is almost always made of wood (either poles or sawn timber), upright posts may be built from bricks or blocks and mortar instead of timber. Precast concrete pillars and metal poles (including decorative cast iron or aluminium ones) may also be used. Screens, on the other hand, can be made from a wide variety of materials, ranging from perforated concrete blocks to wooden latticework or metal. Choose the materials carefully, and ensure that you have the necessary skills to erect the structure before you start.

Roofing

The material, if any, used to cover a pergola will depend on the amount of shade and shelter required, but the visual effect must also be considered. Fibreglass sheeting and corrugated iron will protect you from the rain, but as you will need to build a more substantial roof structure to support these materials, they will not suit all garden styles. Plants will look pretty, but they will only provide shade.

Fabric Various fabrics are suitable for covering both pergolas and screens, but it is best to choose something that is durable. Canvas is reasonably water resistant and is available in a wide range of colours. Shadecloth, a synthetic awning fabric which is also manufactured in various colours and densities, will filter the sun and prevent hail damage, but will not shield you from the rain. It is, however a better option for screens that most other fabrics as it is durable and easy to clean. Waterproof tarpaulin is another possibility. All these materials may be attached directly to the structure, or used for fixed or retractable awnings.

Sheeting Fibrecement, fibreglass and metal sheeting can all be used for pergola roofs. Since purlins (or rafters) will be necessary to support any of these materials, the structure of the pergola will have to be more substantial. Most sheeting should be predrilled and attached to the structure with ring-shanked roofing screws.

Thatch A pergola built from poles could be given a thatched roof, but a pitch of at least 45° is recommended.

Tiles These are used more frequently for gazebos than for pergolas, but if you want to tile a pergola roof, you will have to construct a framework pitched at a minimum of 15°, with beams, rafters and narrow battens to support the tiles.

Timber Lath ceilings and latticework make attractive additions to many pergola designs. Even a simple trellis, designed to be covered with climbing plants, is an option worth considering. These materials are also well suited to screens. Logs or poles, reeds and bamboo may also be used.

Transparent materials In some instances, you may want to shield a deck or patio from the wind but do not want to block the view. The answer here is to erect glass or clear polycarbonate panels. You can make the supports and frames from wood, or buy aluminium ones.

A modest gazebo offers shelter on a large jetty, while the lattice screen gives a feeling of privacy.

A retractable canvas awning has been fitted to a pergola constructed over a timber deck.

LATTICE SCREEN

Making an open lattice screen from timber laths is an elementary project which can easily be tackled with simple hand tools. This design is suitable for screening a small patio or, if erected in place of a railing, a timber deck. First decide where the screen is to be sited, as this will affect its size. For stability, the screen illustrated in this project is attached to a low wall at the side of a slightly elevated patio which is 1.65 m (5 ft 6 in) long, and the top of the panel aligns with an adjacent window frame 2.41 m (8 ft) above ground level. If a patio screen is to be freestanding, a post anchor support system should be concreted into the ground in order to secure the upright timbers adequately. If you adapt the screen for a deck, lengthen the vertical posts and attach them to the decking surface in the same way as you would attach railings (see pages 44-45).

STEP 1

Uprights

3. Position the two upright posts, predrill and secure with Rawl bolts. One of these posts is bolted on to the wall of the house, and the other, which is slightly longer because of the drainage slope to the floor, is bolted to the 350 mm (1 ft 2 in) high wall of the elevated patio. Alternatively, bolt to the deck or attach to the post anchors as described on page 43.

Materials

2 x 2.6 m x 96 mm x 70 mm (8 ft 6 in
   x 3¾ in x 2¾ in) lengths of timber
4 x 2.2 m x 44 mm x 44 mm (7 ft 3 in
   x 1¾ in x 1¾ in) lengths of timber
25 x 2.2 m x 44 mm x 10 mm (7 ft 3 in
   x 1¾ in x ½ in) laths
8 x 12 mm x 150 mm (½ in x 6 in)
   Rawl bolts OR 2 post anchors
   with bolts
8 x 100 mm (4 in) wire nails
54 x 25 mm (1 in) wire nails

Preparation

1. Cut the wood for the framework and the laths to size with a tenon saw.

2. If you are using a post anchor system to secure the posts, you will have to dig holes for the footings, approximately 300 mm x 300 mm x 300 mm (12 in x 12 in x 12 in) in size. Then pour a 1:4:4 cement:sand:stone mix of concrete, and set the bases in the concrete (see page 42). You could also concrete the posts directly into the ground; you will, however, need lengths up to 500 mm (1 ft 8 in) longer if you do this.

This raised patio originally lacked definition and was too small to be fully functional.

STEP 4

Latticework

4. Since the latticework is best assembled flat on the ground, work on a clean, flat area, such as paving. Join the 44 mm x 44 mm (1¾ in x 1¾ in) lengths of wood at right angles, using corner clamps to hold them, and nail them together so that they form a rectangle. Ensure that the corners are at exactly 90°.

STEP 5

5. Now attach the laths to the framework at 144 mm (5½ in) centres, using the shorter nails. First nail the horizontal slats, including one each directly onto the top and bottom pieces of the framework. Then nail the vertical slats, omitting the

Not only does the screen conceal an adjacent utility area, but it is a feature in itself.

two end slats where the screen will be attached to the upright posts. The latticework may be spaced according to the degree of privacy or protection you require. This design has a 100 mm (4 in) grid; if you want smaller squares, you will simply need more laths. Bear in mind, though, that while a smaller grid size will result in a more rigid screen, it can become visually intrusive if erected in a small space.

Attaching the screen

6. Position the screen against the upright posts, ensuring that the entire structure is square, level and plumb. Use a spirit level to do this accurately.

7. Nail the screen to the posts with the longer nails. Once the screen is securely in position, cut the excess wood off the tops of the posts with a hand saw.

STEP 8

Finishing

8. The finished screen may be varnished, painted or coated with a penetrating oil preservative dressing. This is especially important if you are planning to use it as a trellis for plants, as the wood will not be accessible once it is covered with plant growth. In this case a UV-resistant and weatherproof exterior varnish was painted on to the screen.

STEP 6

STEP 7

PERGOLA FOR SHADE

Bricklaying skills and a basic knowledge of carpentry are required for this pergola project. A simple structure, it is attached to the corner of the house and shades an area of 26.25 m² (32 sq yd). Pillars are made of bricks and plaster. Beams of sawn and planed timber are fixed to the house with truss hangers, so there is no need to knock out any brickwork to attach them. Shadecloth was chosen as the roof covering, as it filters sunlight, although any other awning material could be used instead.

Materials
384 plaster bricks
210 kg (465 lb) cement
0.65 m³ (¾ cu yd) sand
300 kg (660 lb) stone
20 kg (45 lb) lime (optional)
5 x 3.5 m x 144 mm x 44 mm (11 ft 6 in x 5½ in x 1¾ in) lengths of timber
3 x 3.75 m x 144 mm x 44 mm (12 ft 4 in x 5½ in x 1¾ in) lengths of timber
2 x 3.85 m x 144 mm x 44 mm (12 ft 8 in x 5½ in x 1¾ in) lengths of timber
3 x 2.5 m x 44 mm x 10 mm (8 ft 2 in x 1¾ in x ½ in) cover strips
2 x 3.75 m x 44 mm x 10 mm (12 ft 4 in x 1¾ in x ½ in) cover strips (optional)
2 x 3.5 m x 44 mm x 10 mm (11 ft 6 in x 1¾ in x ½ in) cover strips (optional)
11 m x 3 m (12 yd x 120 in) shadecloth or awning material
12 m (39 ft 6 in) galvanised iron strapping
20 x 100 mm (4 in) coach screws
5 x 50 mm (2 in) truss hangers
10 x 8 mm x 50 mm (⅜ in x 2 in) Rawl bolts
5 x 75 mm (3 in) hexagonal bolts with nuts and washers
26 x 75 mm (3 in) wire nails
heavy-duty staples or shadecloth fasteners

Preparation
1. When building a pergola on an existing patio, remove pavers to accommodate footings for the pillars. Use a chisel and club hammer to chip away the brick. Where a pillar is to be built on an unpaved surface, remove all vegetation.

Footings
2. Dig four holes as shown in the diagram on page 84, approximately 400 mm (1 ft 4 in) deep and 650 mm x 500 mm (2 ft x 1 ft 8 in) across – they should be big enough to support 2.4 m (7 ft 10 in) high pillars built with three bricks in each course. The corners of the footings should be square.

3. Insert a peg into the centre of each footing to indicate the upper level of the concrete. You will need about 45 kg (100 lb) of cement for the concrete, which you should mix in a cement:sand:stone ratio of 1:3:4.

STEP 4

4. Pour the concrete mixture into each hole to the height of the peg. Divide the strapping into four equal lengths by bending it back and forth until it snaps. Bend one end of each length of strapping and sink one into each of the wet concrete footings. Allow the concrete to set for at least 24 to 48 hours. The strapping will

The patio before the paving was extended (see pages 57-58) and the pergola constructed.

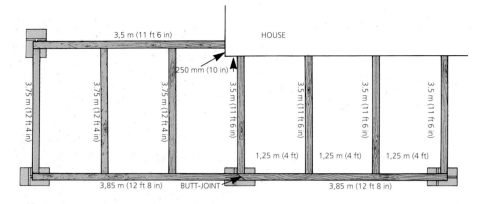

Diagram labels:
3,5 m (11 ft 6 in)   HOUSE
3,75 m (12 ft 4 in)   3,75 m (12 ft 4 in)   3,75 m (12 ft 4 in)   3,5 m (11 ft 6 in)   3,5 m (11 ft 6 in)   3,5 m (11 ft 6 in)   3,5 m (11 ft 6 in)
250 mm (10 in)
1,25 m (4 ft)   1,25 m (4 ft)   1,25 m (4 ft)
3,85 m (12 ft 8 in)   BUTT-JOINT   3,85 m (12 ft 8 in)

of cement to do this. You may have to add lime to improve the plasticity, cohesiveness and water retention of the mixture. Using a screed board to hold the mixture as you work, lay on the plaster or render with a plasterer's trowel, applying pressure to make it stick to the bricks. Leave for about an hour, then smooth with a plasterer's float.

STEP 9

9. Splash a little water on the surface and use a steel float to get a smooth finish. Use a corner trowel to neaten the corners.

10. The plastered or rendered surface should not be allowed to dry out too quickly. Damp it down every now and then with a very fine spray of water for two or three days. Allow it to dry thoroughly before painting.

help to reinforce the pillars and may be used to hold the pergola beams in place. More substantial pillars will require metal reinforcing rods, and shorter lengths of strapping can be built into the top five or six courses.

rod or water level to check that the brick courses and mortar joints are even. For a 2.4 m (7 ft 10 in) pillar, you will need to lay 30-32 courses, depending on how deep the foundation is and how many courses are below the level of the paving.

STEP 5

Building the pillars
5. Mix cement and sand in the ratio 1:4 for mortar. Lay the bricks so that the strapping extends through the middle of the pillar, with two bricks side-by-side and a third longways at one end. For the next course, alternate the direction of the bricks by laying one to overlap half of the two laid side-by-side and two more to cover the rest of the surface. This will facilitate proper bonding. Fill all brick holes and gaps between the bricks with mortar as you work.

6. It is essential to build the pillars so that corners are at 90°, so use a builder's square frequently to check this. Also use a spirit level to ensure that each course is level and the pillars are plumb.

7. Set up corner blocks (see pages 10 and 22) and a builder's line to help ensure that brick courses are even. String a builder's line between the pillars, and use a gauge

STEP 7

Plastering or rendering the pillars
8. Once the brickwork is completed, allow the mortar to set at least overnight before plastering or rendering. Mix the plaster or render in the same ratio as the mortar (1:4); you will need at least 40 kg (90 lb)

STEP 8

STEP 11

Positioning the timbers
11. Once the pillars are dry, you can erect the timber beams. First mark the position of the truss hangers on the wall. Ensure that they are equally spaced and positioned exactly opposite each pillar (see diagram), or the beams will be off-centre where they are attached to the pillars. If the patio is about 7.5 m (24 ft) long, the hangers

should be at 1.25 (4 ft) centres. Use a water level to check the height of the truss hangers against the height of the tops of the columns (see page 10).

12. Drill holes for the Rawl bolts, and bolt the truss hangers to the wall, ensuring that they are absolutely level.

13. Double-check the distance between the truss hangers and the three pillars. If your measuring was accurate, there should be no problems. It is usually wise, though, to buy timber a little longer than required. It is easy to cut a piece off the beam; frustrating to find that the beam is too short.

STEP 17

STEP 14.

14. Carefully lower the first 3.5 m (11 ft 6 in) crosspiece into position. One end will slot into the truss hanger and be secured with a hexagonal bolt, while the other will rest on the pillar and be screwed to the abutting beam later on.

15. Cut one end of each 3.85 m (12 ft 8 in) beam at a 45° angle. Position the first beam so that it is at right angles to the first crosspiece, and the angled end rests on the middle pillar.

16. Drill holes through the beam into the first crosspiece, and hammer in two coach screws, using a spanner or ratchet to tighten the nuts.

17. Punch a hole in the strapping, wrap it over the beam and nail it down.

18. Position the second 3.85 m (12 ft 8 in) beam to form a diagonal butt joint (see diagram on page 84) with the first, and skew-nail the two together.

19. Position the end 3.75 m (12 ft 4 in) crosspiece and secure the two timbers at 90° with coach screws and strapping, as in steps 16 and 17.

20. Now secure the last beam to the crosspiece and pillar with coach screws and strapping, and slot the other end into the truss hanger.

21. Use a spirit level to ensure that each piece of timber is exactly straight and level.

STEP 21

22. Returning to the central pillar, nail the strapping over the diagonal butt joint.

23. Secure the three remaining 3.5 m (11 ft 6 in) crosspieces, slotting one end of each into a truss hanger and bolting it, and securing the other end to the beam with coach screws as before.

24. The two remaining 3.75 m (12 ft 4 in) crosspieces are secured at each end with two coach screws.

Finishing the wood
25. If you are going to paint the structure or varnish the wood, do so now. If you plan to paint the truss hangers, remember to coat them with a suitable primer first.

Attaching the awning material
26. Since the timbers are set at about 1.25 m (4 ft) centres, the material will have to be trimmed to about 2.5 m (8 ft 3 in) wide so that the material joins lie along the crosspieces. If you are using shadecloth, cut it with a soldering iron to prevent it from fraying.

STEP 27

27. Wrap one end of the shadecloth around a cover strip or any other narrow length of timber and attach it with tacks, staples or shadecloth fasteners. This will help you to keep it taut and in place. With the cover strip and the fasteners on the upper side of the shadecloth, nail the cover strip across the first three crosspieces, above the truss hangers and as close to the wall as possible.

28. Pull the material taut across the structure, securing it along each of the three beams with staples or fasteners. Use a second strip of timber on the other end of the material to help keep the shadecloth in position and to neaten the edge. Repeat twice to cover the entire pergola, overlapping the lengths slightly at the joins. If your pergola fits around the corner of the house, you will have to cut the awning fabric to follow the shape of the wall, and divide one piece of 2.5 m (8 ft 2 in) cover strip into two shorter lengths.

29. Trim the shadecloth along the edge of the beam with a soldering iron.

30. When all the shadecloth is in place, you can secure it with additional lengths of cover strip along the joins if you wish.

STEP 28

STEP 29

The pillars have been painted white and the timber black, in keeping with the design and style of the house.

PATIO SCREEN WALL

If your patio is exposed to prevailing winds, a screen wall will provide welcome protection, and will enable you to make greater use of your outdoor area. This project, which is suitable for anyone with basic bricklaying skills, features a brick wall which not only shields the patio on windy days, but also creates some privacy from the neighbouring property. It is not high enough, however, to hide the lovely mountain views. The hole in the wall is a feature which may be used to display plants, an urn or a garden sculpture, for instance, which should ideally be cemented into place for stability.

Materials

For a screen wall 1 m (3 ft 3 in) high and about 2 m (6 ft 6 in) long:
113 facebricks
11 paving bricks
30 kg (65 lb) cement
120 kg (270 lb) sand
1 m (3 ft 3 in) reinforcing

Preparation

1. This wall was built as an extension to an existing one-brick patio wall, which was 400 mm (1 ft 4 in) high. In a case such as this, simply make sure that the surface is sound and clean before you start laying the additional bricks.

If you are starting from scratch, however, dig a trench and throw a strip foundation for the wall. For a half-brick wall, up to about a metre (3 ft) in height, this should be about 200 mm (8 in) wide and 100 mm (4 in) deep, and you should use a 1:4:4 cement:sand:stone mix. If you want the wall to be higher than a metre (3 ft), rather build a one-brick wall, for which the foundation will have to be more substantial (see page 15), and the mix should be slightly stronger – about 1:3:4. You will also need to buy more bricks, cement and sand (see pages 12-14).

Building the wall and piers

2. Using a clean tin or bucket to measure cement and sand, mix mortar in the ratio 1:4. Lay the bricks in a straight line to form a stretcher bond. Corner blocks and a builder's line will help you to keep each course straight, but use a spirit level frequently to check all planes of the brickwork as the wall progresses.

3. Even though this is a very short wall, you will need a one-brick pier at each end. Bricklaying methods for building a pillar are clearly illustrated in previous projects, particularly on pages 83-84. Since these piers are very low, reinforcing is not required. Place a strip of mortar on the uppermost surface of the wall, butter the end of a brick and then press it firmly into place. Tap the brick with the trowel handle to level it, and scrape off any excess mortar. It is important to be as neat as possible when laying facebricks – it can be an arduous task cleaning up badly pointed bricks at a later stage. As you lay the bricks, scrape the trowel upwards against the wall surface to remove the mortar.

4. Lay the first four courses on top of the existing wall, stepping the brickwork up to the corners. Use a gauge rod to check that brick courses are even and a builder's square to ensure that the corners of the piers remain at 90°.

5. Lay another five courses, leaving a gap two bricks wide where the hole will be. To edge off the hole, you will have to halve some bricks (see page 25). Stack

STEP 2

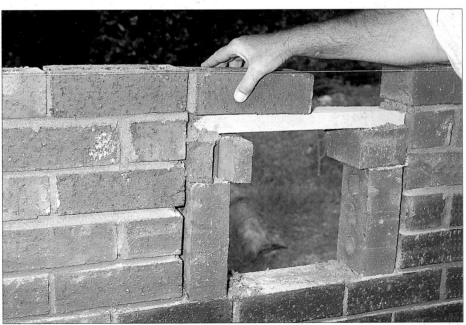

STEP 5

extra bricks in the gap and place a piece of wood, the width of the hole, across the top, leaving a hole four courses high. Lay the next two bricks over the timber.

6. To strengthen the opening in the wall, it is essential to place reinforcing on the bricks which cover the gap in the brickwork. Put mortar over this and then continue laying the bricks as before, until there are 11 courses of brickwork.

Finishing

7. Use a pointing trowel or piece of metal to rake out the joints. Finish off the top of the wall with a course of paving bricks.

8. Leave the mortar to dry for at least 24 hours, then remove the loose bricks and the piece of wood.

STEP 6

STEP 7

STEP 8

The completed screen wall shields part of the patio from wind and creates a private seating area.

FINISHING TOUCHES

Having constructed your deck or patio, you will be faced with the challenge of furnishing and decorating it. Outdoor furniture not only provides you with a place to sit – it can also lend style and a feeling of intimacy to the area. Lighting, while essentially practical, can add a magical dimension too, while pots and planters will brighten up dull, awkward corners.

After the physical demands of working with bricks and mortar, concrete or timber, adding the finishing touches can be a creative and relaxing task. Well chosen and placed, lighting, furniture and ornaments will give your patio or deck atmosphere, and will encourage you to make full use of your new outdoor area.

Lighting

Although it is an essential element of all outdoor living areas, lighting is frequently neglected in the planning stages of a building project such as a deck or patio. This can mean losing the opportunity to bury unsightly cables under paving or low-level decking.

If your patio is attached to the house, existing fittings on exterior walls may be quite adequate. If not, you will have to select lights or lamps which are suitable for outdoor use.

While many of the fittings chosen for the garden are designed for decorative purposes, such as highlighting foliage or creating a moody glow, you will need something more practical on a patio. It is often preferable to aim for reasonably general lighting, such as wall-mounted fittings, or lamps set on top of a pillar or post. If the area is right next to the house and has a solid roof structure, you can even use freestanding lamps. Spotlights are useful for casting a direct shaft of light over a cooking or eating area.

Coloured lights are often favoured for patios, and strung around a barbecue or alfresco eating area, they will certainly add a festive air. You could even use paraffin or oil lanterns, or slow-burning garden candles mounted on sticks.

Seating

The convenience and practicality of furniture, both permanent and movable, cannot be underestimated in outdoor living spaces. Without it, the area will simply not be fully functional.

A yellow awning matches cushions on practical, plastic garden furniture.

If you prefer the idea of permanent seating, it is best to include this when designing your deck or patio, rather than adding on later – seating built from bricks and mortar or stone requires a solid foundation (see page 20), while timber benches on a deck should ideally be bolted to the joists or beams.

If portable chairs and tables are your choice, the possibilities are virtually endless, although not all kinds may be left outdoors indefinitely. Precast concrete, plastic, cast-iron and hardwood chairs and benches are all suitable. Most lighter metal furniture, canvas chairs, or cane and wicker should be stored indoors and carried outside when required.

Of course, the type of seating chosen ought to be in keeping with the style of your house and garden, and should reflect the mood you wish to create. As a rule, materials and finishes should also suit those used for the deck or patio itself.

Containers for planting

Whatever material you have chosen for the flooring, it may look bleak or bland unless you soften hard lines and add colour with plants. There are several ways of doing this, such as establishing beds at the edge or including built-in planters (see page 53).

Less permanent but often more striking, plants in pots, tubs and other containers will add life and colour to any deck, patio or courtyard. The effect may be further enhanced if containers are grouped together. The type of container you use should be compatible in shape and size with whatever you plan to plant. Instead of buying containers, you could construct timber planters (see pages 92-93), or if pottery is one of your hobbies, you could make your own pots to suit your deck or patio and your plants. Otherwise, many charming terracotta and concrete designs are available, as well as fibrecement pots which can be painted for an individual look. You may prefer to use recycled containers – old wine barrels, chimney pots, baths and sinks are all possibilities.

Remember that good drainage, regular watering and feeding are all essential for your plants' well-being. For drainage purposes, even the smallest pot should have at least one hole in its base, and stones should be set beneath the soil.

Ornaments

Statues and other ornaments should be chosen and positioned with care. Wall-mounted plaques and panels are particularly well-suited to patios and courtyards which have solidly constructed screen walls or are attached to the house. Spouting fountains (which can also be mounted on a wall) are popular, although, like niches and alcoves, they will usually have to be part of the initial design.

The size of statues and sculptures will depend on the dimensions of the patio, and attention should be given to their positioning. One well-placed piece could become a focal point, while with too much ornamentation you run the risk of the area looking somewhat cluttered.

Moveable garden chairs are a practical option for seating under a thatched umbrella.

Elegant metal furniture, a canvas umbrella and potted plants add style to a patio built next to a pool deck.

Awning material shades a deck and adds colour.

Elegant furniture and a selection of pots give character to a small patio.

Potted plants and attractive metal furniture with soft cushions and bows, add style and colour to a covered patio.

WOODEN PLANTER

While most planters made from wood are simply variations on the basic box, there are numerous ways to enhance the surface area. Add timber decoration in the form of raised vertical or horizontal bands, or use paint. However, your design does not have to be complicated to be effective – this easy project is perfect for an inexperienced carpenter, and filled with flowers or shrubs, it will brighten up your patio or deck.

STEP 4

Materials
28 x 396 mm x 44 mm x 44 mm
  (1 ft 2 in x 2 in x 2 in) pieces of wood
4 x 440 mm x 110 mm x 22 mm
  (1 ft 4 in x 4 in x 1 in) planks
4 x 310 mm x 44 mm x 44 mm (12 in
  x 2 in x 2 in) pieces of wood
118 x 75 mm (3 in) wire nails
20 x 50 mm (2 in) wire nails
wood glue

STEP 1

Preparation
1. Cut the wood to size before you start work. If you do not have a power saw, use an ordinary tenon saw.

2. Place the first four pieces of wood on a flat, stable surface, and use a builder's square to check that the corners are at right angles.

Construction
3. Start gluing and nailing the box together, using the 75 mm (3 in) wire nails. To connect the wood, ensure that

STEP 2

the ends of the pieces of timber overlap each other at the corners. Put wood glue on the surface and push the wood firmly onto it. If the glue dribbles, wipe off the excess with a cloth or tissue.

STEP 3

4. Clamp each corner with a right-angled clamp before gluing and nailing the second and subsequent layers. It is wise to predrill the holes to prevent the wood from splitting, making sure that the nail holes are not directly above each other.

5. Hammer the nails flush with the surface. If the wood is warped, you may have to use sash clamps during the gluing and pinning process to hold the layers of timber together while the glue dries.

6. When you have glued and nailed seven layers of wood, nail on the base, using the 50 mm (2 in) nails. If you have cut the wood accurately, the planks will fit exactly; if not, trim the planks or cut another piece to size. Insert two nails at the end of each plank and two or three along the two remaining sides of the base.

STEP 6

7. Now nail the four 310 mm (12 in) pieces of wood to the base, using the 50 mm (2 in) nails, with their outer edges 44 mm (2 in) in from the edges of the box. These will keep the planter off the ground and enhance the final design.

STEP 7

Finishing

8. Fill in nail holes, imperfections in the wood and gaps between the timbers with a wood filler that matches the colour of the wood. Sand the surface when dry.

STEP 8

9. Drill holes in the base of the planter for drainage.

10. Seal the inside of the box with bitumen. This black emulsion waterproofer is simply painted on, but it should be spread reasonably thickly to be effective. You can also seal the underside of the planter.

STEP 10

11. Finally paint the box, or give it a coat of diluted emulsion paint for a washed or slightly distressed look. If you plan to display it on your deck, varnish it to match the finish of the timber.

Painted and stencilled, the wooden planter is an ideal container for pink roses and strawberry plants.

LIST OF SUPPLIERS

AUSTRALIA

Mitre 10 (NSW) Ltd
122 Newton Road
Wetherill Park NSW 2164
Tel: (02) 725 3222
(Branches throughout Australia)

BBC Hardware Stores (Head Office)
P O Box 201
Parramatta 2124
Tel: (02) 683 888
(Branches throughout Australia)

NEW ZEALAND

Carter Holt Builders Supplies
Head office: Tel: (09) 849 4153
(Branches throughout Auckland)

Placemakers
Head office: Tel: (09) 303 0299
(Branches throughout New Zealand)

The Building Depot
Head office: Tel: (09) 827 0905
(Branches throughout Auckland)

Exotic Building Supplies
Head office: Tel: (09) 274 5755
(Branches throughout Auckland)

Benchmark Building Supplies
Head office: Tel: (09) 815 1506
(Branches throughout New Zealand)

UNITED KINGDOM

B & Q plc
Portswood House
Hampshire Corporate Park
Chandlers Ford
Eastleigh
Hants
SO5 3YX
Tel: (0703) 256256
(Branches throughout the UK)

Bypass Nurseries
72 Ipswich Road
Colchester
CO1 2YF
Tel: (0206) 865500
(for plants and garden accessories)

Do-It-All
Falcon House
The Minories
Dudley
West Midlands
DY2 8PG
Tel: (0384) 456456
(Branches throughout the UK)

Harcross Timber and Building Supplies
1 Great Tower Street
London
EC3R 5AH
Tel: (071) 711 1444

Jewson Ltd
Intwood Road
Cringleford
Norwich
NR4 UXB
Tel: (0603) 56133
(Branches throughout the UK)

Texas Homecare
Homecharm House
Parkfarm
Wellingborough
Northampton
Tel: (0933) 679679
(Branches throughout the UK)

Travis Perkins
Lodge Way House
Lodge Way
Harlestone Road
Northampton
NN5 7UG
Tel: (0604) 752424
(Branches throughout the UK)

Wickes
120-138 Station Road
Harrow
Middlesex
HA1 2QB
Tel: (081) 863 5696
(Branches throughout the UK)

Homebase Ltd
Beddington House
Wallington
Surrey
Tel: (081) 784 7200
(Branches throughout the UK)

GLOSSARY

Aggregate Sand, gravel or crushed stone which is mixed with cement to make mortar or concrete, respectively. In Britain a mixture of sand and gravel (hoggin) is known as all-in aggregate. In South Africa all-in aggregate refers to an inferior material which should not be used.

Anodise Electro-chemical process used to coat metal with a protective film. Common treatment for aluminium.

Auger Machine or hand tool used to bore holes in the ground.

Bitumen Tarlike substance used to protect and waterproof timber which will be directly exposed to moisture.

Bond Various related methods used to ensure that brick courses overlap, thus increasing the strength of a wall. Your choice of brick bond will depend on the effect you wish to achieve.

Blocking Method used to brace joists in deck substructure.

Buttering Technique used to apply mortar or adhesive to tiles or bricks.

Cantilever Building system used, for example, to attach a deck to a building without upright posts extending to ground level. Steps may also be cantilevered.

Cleat Wedge of wood attached to the stringers of a staircase to support treads of some step designs. Longer cleats are also used when attaching panelling to internal walls.

Cobble Stone or precast block which may be used to form patio surface.

Concrete A mixture of cement, sand, crushed stone or gravel and water used for foundations, steps, paths and so on.

Course A continuous row of bricks. Several courses form a wall, pillar or other brick structure.

Curing Chemical reaction between concrete and water which results in the strengthening of concrete as it hardens.

Damp-proof course (DPC) Layer of impervious material, used to minimise damp in buildings. It is laid under the floor slab and in the walls of buildings, and where a patio adjoins a house. When laid under paving, it inhibits weed growth.

Engawa Traditional Japanese deck constructed around the house.

Facebrick Clay or concrete brick manufactured for use without plaster.

Fascia Boarding erected to hide the deck structure. Also refers to timbers affixed to rafters used to neaten a roof.

Flashing Waterproofing material used to stop rain and other moisture from penetrating between a ledger and the walls of a house. Also used to seal around chimneys, dormer windows and so on.

Footing Projecting course at foot of wall. Term also used with reference to foundations, particularly of pillars and piers.

Formwork Shuttering used to contain wet concrete cast on site.

Galvanise Method used to coat iron with zinc to stop it from rusting.

Grout Thin mortar mixture or similar material used to fill gaps between tiles.

Hardcore Various materials including broken bricks, stone and other rubble compacted to provide a solid surface beneath a concrete slab or patio floor.

Hardwood Botanical classification identifying broadleafed species.

Header Brick laid with its face at right angles to the wall. Also refers to the head or short side of a brick.

Hot tub Traditionally made from Californian redwood, hot tubs incorporate jets, pumps, filters and heaters like those found in spas.

Joists Parallel timbers laid on edge under decking slats.

Lath Narrow strip of timber used for trellises, latticework or as part of the roof of an overhead structure.

Lattice (or latticework) Criss-cross structure of laths; often used for screens.

Ledger Horizontal timber attached to the face of a building to support beams or joists of a deck structure. Similar support timbers attached to beams for joists to rest on are also called ledgers.

Mortar A mixture of cement and sand used to bind bricks or stones together.

Pergola Arbour, covered walk or overhead structure built to give shade or shelter to a patio or deck.

Piling Post or heavy beam driven vertically into soft sand as support for deck or other structure. A pile foundation, sometimes necessary on a steep slope, involves filling holes bored into the ground with reinforced concrete to form a strong support base for deck pillars or posts.

Plaster A mixture of cement and sand, and sometimes lime, used to cover brickwork. In some countries, this is called render when applied outdoors. Also refers to the application of plaster.

Post anchor Metal base set in a concrete foundation to anchor timber posts. Used in various building structures including pergolas and decks.

Punner Ramming tool used to compact earth or hardcore.

Rawlbolts Heavy-duty expanding bolts used to attach timber and other materials to brick and concrete surfaces.

Render Refers to the first coat of plaster used to cover brickwork.

Riser The vertical surface between each tread of a step.

Sand, sharp or soft As the fine aggregate in concrete, mortar and plaster mixes, sand is graded. Coarse or 'sharp' sand should be used for concrete, and 'soft' building sand for mortar. Plaster sand may contain extra lime. In some areas only one grade of builder's sand may be available for all aspects of a project.

Screed Mixture of cement, sand and water laid over a rough concrete slab. Essential for concrete slabs which are to be tiled.

Sett A square block of stone, traditionally granite, used for paving.

Shuttering Framework erected as a temporary support for concrete cast in situ.

Skew-nail/skew-screw Method of driving nails or screws into any timber at an angle.

Softwood Botanical classification identifying coniferous species.

Spa Made from acrylic material or concrete cast in situ, hot-water spas have air and water jets and their own pump and filter. Although used for hydrotherapy and often located indoors, they are frequently built into patio areas.

Spacer Length or block of timber used to keep lengths of wood apart in a regular manner. Often used to separate two posts which form a single upright which supports a deck or pergola structure.

Stretcher Bricks laid with sides in face of wall. Also refers to the long face of a brick. In stretcher-bond walls, all bricks are laid as stretchers, with each brick overlapping two beneath by half a length.

Stringer Sloping timber, positioned edge side up, used on either side of a stairway to support the steps.

Tread The flat, upper surface of a step.

Trellis Lattice or criss-cross wooden, metal or wire structure used for screening or to support plants.

Verandah Patio attached to a house; usually raised and often covered by a form of roofing material.

INDEX

A

aggregate 14
angle brackets 18
angle grinders 11
angled decks 30, 36
attached decks 29
auger 10
awning fabric 80
awnings 85–86

B

beams 34, 42, 84–85
bits 11
block splitters 11
blocking 34, 35
bolts 18
bonds
    for paving 23, 24
    in brickwork 23
bracing 35
bradawl 11
bricklaying 22–23, 68–69, 70,
    83–86, 87–88
brick piers 34, 87
brick pillars 84
bricks and blocks 12–13
    cutting 25
    for patio flooring 49
bridges 31
builder's line 10
butt joints 27

C

cantilevered decks 30–31
carpentry 25–27, 38–40,
    41–45, 75–76, 81–82, 83–86,
    92–93
cement 13
chisels 11
clamps 12
cobbles 50, 61–62
cold chisel 11
compactors 10–11
concrete 32
    materials for 13–15
    precast 12–13
    working with 20–22
concrete blocks 70–71
concrete columns 33
concrete mixers 11
connectors 17–18, 26–27
costs 9
cut and fill 20
cutting
    bricks and pavers 25
    tiles 64
    timber 26

D

damp–proof course 20
decking slats 35
decks
    construction of 32–36
    types of 29–32

design and style 6–7
    for decks 28
    for overheads and screens 79
    for pathways 67
    for patios 46–48
    for steps 66–67
drainage 20
drills 11

E

edging 23, 24, 55, 58

F

facebricks 68–69
fascia boards 35
fasteners 17–18, 26–27
files 12
finishing
    brickwork 88
    cobbles or setts 62
    concrete steps 71
    flagstones 60
    paving 56, 58, 69
    precast concrete 74
    tiling 64
    timber 17, 40, 45, 54, 76, 82,
        85, 93
flagstones 50, 59–60
floats 11
flooring
    for decks 28
    for patios 48–50
footings 83–84
formwork 21
foundations 42, 52, 68, 70, 87
furniture 89
framework, for decks 36, 38,
    43–44

G

gazebos see overhead structures
grouting 64

H

hammers 11

J

Japanese–style decks 30
jetties 31
joins, for timber 27
jointers 11
joist hangers 18, 34

L

laminated timber 16
lap joint 27
latticework 82
ledgers 34
level 19–20
levels 10
lighting 89
lime 15
location 6–7
low–level decks 29, 38–40

M

materials 12–18
    for decks 32
    for pathways 67
    for roofing and screens 80
    for steps 67
measuring, timber 26
metal reinforcing devices 18
mortar 13–15, 22
    cleaning 25
mortarboards 11
multilevel decks 29

N

nails 17
notching 27

O

ornaments 90
overhead structures 79–80, 83–86

P

paint 17
paths 67, 77
patterns, for paving 23, 24
pavers 12–13
    cutting 25
paving 23–25, 49–50, 69
    flexible 24, 52–54
    hybrid 25, 55–56
    maintenance of 25
    rigid 24–25, 57–58
pergolas see overhead structures
pick 10
plane 12
planters 53, 70, 74, 89–90, 92–93
plaster 13–15
plastering 23, 71, 84
plasticiser 15
pliers 12
plumb 20
plumb bob 10
pointing tools 11
poles 16, 33
pool deck 29–30, 41–45
post anchors 18, 33, 39–40, 43
    steel 34
precast concrete 50, 72–74
preservatives 16–17
professionals 7–9
punners 10–11

Q

quantities, estimating 12–15,
    22, 50

R

railings 28, 36, 44–45
railway sleepers 50
ramming tools 10–11
rasps 12
rendering see plastering
retaining wall 20, 72–73
roofing 79–80

S

sand 13–14
sanders 12
sawn timber 16
saws 11
screed 24, 63
screedboards 11
screens 81–82, 87–88
screwdrivers 11
screws 17
seating 53, 89
setting out 19, 41–42
setts 50, 61–62
sheeting 80
shovels 10
slate 50
spa deck 29–30
spacers 10
spades 10
spanners 12
square 19
squares 10
staples 17
stepping stones 77
steps 66–67, 68–69, 70–71,
    72–74, 75–76
stone 14–15

T

tape measure, retractable 10
thatch 80
tile–cutting machines 11
tiling
    for flooring 50, 63–65
    for roofing 80
timber 15–17 see also carpentry
    connecting 26–27
    cutting 26
    defects in 15, 16
    for decks 32
    for flooring 50
    for overheads and screens 80
    maintenance of 36
    measuring 26
    types of 32
tools 10–12
transparent roofing 80
trowels 11

U

upright supports 33, 81
    connections for 34

V

varnish 17

W

walls 12, 68, 87–88, see also
    retaining walls
water 13
water level 19–20
wheelbarrows 10
wood see timber
work–benches 12